MORE PRAISE FOR

DR. SUSAN BIALI AND
LIVE A LIFE YOU LOVE

"The book is a beautifully-written and rare melding of memoir, science, and experience-based guidance in self-empowerment. Dr. Biali has provided the gear and compass to the road less traveled."

—ALAN C. LOGAN, ND, FRSH, Author of *The Brain Diet*

"Susan Biali is the real deal. Her life experiences and enthusiasm make her a credible and powerful force to help us all create health, happiness, and passion in our lives. Thank you, Susan!"

—DIANE SIEG, RN, CYT, CSP, Speaker, Author,
Life Coach, Yoga Teacher, Creator of *30 Days to Grace*

"Dr. Susan Biali's refreshing enthusiasm for life shines through in her informative and entertaining writing . . . her inspiration is both engaging and infectious."

—RICK CAMPBELL, Editor & Associate Publisher, *The Medical Post*

"Susan Biali is one of the most inspirational individuals I know. *Live a Life You Love*, with Susan's uplifting story and practical steps, is a must read for anyone who has an inner desire to experience more passion and fulfillment in their lives."

—TERESIA LAROCQUE, Master Certified Coach and Professional Speaker

"Dr. Susan Biali's story is remarkable and unique . . . her message transcends gender and cultures."

—BRITTA STROMEYER ESMAIL, Feature Writer, Suite 101.com

"Dr. Biali is an amazing physician, life coach, and wellness expert. Her background in nutrition and medicine gives her a great ability to help others achieve healthy eating and a healthier lifestyle."

—Dr. Geoff Rutledge, M.D., Ph.D., Chief Medical Information Officer,
The Health Central Network & Wellsphere.com

"The fact that she has a degree in nutrition, is a medical doctor, and has survived some trying times adds substantial weight to her words . . . judging from her drive and down-to-earth appeal, Biali could well be B.C.'s next wellness star."

—*The Vancouver Sun*

"Medical doctor turned flamenco dancer . . . a woman who has walked her dark nights of the soul, but rather than allowing it to shatter her, has had the courage to move through it and find her place of purpose with grace. Dr. Biali is a total class act and an extraordinary Woman Of Worth."

—CHRISTINE AWRAM, Founder, Woman of Worth (WOW) Events

"I love the way Susan Biali shares her story and really appreciate her values and perspective on life. She is an inspiration for how I want to be as an author, speaker, coach, and person."

—JENNY BLAKE, Career Development Program Manager, Google, and Blogger, *Life After College*

"Susan is an extremely knowledgeable and well-spoken advisor . . . The advice and information she gave was exceptional as she talked about common illnesses that are either work- or stress-related, and how they can be easily changed with some very simple changes to how one lives their life."

—KARL RICHTER, Director, "The Daily" and "The Daily: Weekend Edition"

"A major new writer is calling."

—DANIEL WOOD, author, Winner of 31 regional and national writing awards, and Recipient of the *Western Magazine* Awards Lifetime Achievement Award

"Her innate ability to write . . . gives readers a true insight into healthy and authentic living. I strongly endorse Susan as a talented writer, healthcare professional, and wellness coach."

—BRENDA WOOD, Publisher, *HEART Business Journal for Women*

"Susan Biali is absolutely one-of-a-kind! She walks her talk; lives with courage and passion; and excites everyone who crosses her path to do the same."

—CRYSTAL ANDRUS, Bestselling Author, Radio & TV personality

DR. SUSAN BIALI, M.D.

LIVE A LIFE

You LOVE

7 STEPS TO
A HEALTHIER, HAPPIER,
MORE PASSIONATE YOU

BEAUFORT BOOKS • NEW YORK, NEW YORK

Library of Congress Cataloging-in-Publication Data
Biali, Susan.
 Live a life you love : seven steps to a healthier, happier, more passionate you / Susan
Biali.
    p. cm.
 ISBN 978-0-8253-0599-3 (alk. paper)
 1. Self-acceptance. 2. Body image. 3. Self-realization. I. Title.
 BF575.S37B53 2010
 158.1—dc22
                                        2009036888

For inquiries about volume orders, please contact:
Beaufort Books
27 West 20th Street, Suite 1102
New York, NY 10011
sales@beaufortbooks.com

Published in the United States by Beaufort Books
www.beaufortbooks.com

Distributed by Midpoint Trade Books
www.midpointtrade.com

www.susanbiali.com

Printed in the United States of America

To my parents

Who always told me that I could do anything
I put my mind to, even though they didn't
always agree with what I wanted to do.

CONTENTS

THE TIME IS RIGHT!

WELCOME! IT'S SUCH an honor for me that you're here with me, right now. In my life, the authors of books have been my best friends, my teachers, my mentors, and my biggest cheerleaders. When everyone around me thought that my ideas or dreams were crazy, I always managed to find a book that told me that I was right, that I should have faith in myself and in life, and that everything was possible.

I hope to give you the same gift that other authors have given me. You hold this book in your hands for a reason. Maybe you've been thinking of making some changes in your life, and my stories and suggestions will inspire and guide you into your next steps.

Or perhaps your life is crumbling around you and you don't know what to do next. If that's the case, I hope that my words will take you by the hand and help pull you out of that darkness, back up into the light that's available to all of us.

Regardless of where you're at, your timing is perfect. No matter how old you are, no matter how many mistakes you've made, no matter how much time you've "wasted" in unfruitful thoughts, activities, relationships, or jobs, you are meant to be here with me, right now. It's time!

One day, you'll see how all those "wrong turns" and difficult experiences in your life have worked together to create the perfect you and your perfect life. Right now, *you* are perfectly designed to live, and serve the world, in the way that only you can.

You might not be able to see the perfection in you now, and may doubt that my words could apply to you and your life. That's totally normal. I remember reading books that talked about "finding your purpose," and feeling so frustrated that I hadn't found mine yet. I felt convinced that I would never, ever discover any kind of joyful, meaningful purpose to my life. I also remember reading books about happiness, and doubting that I would ever find that, either.

During those early years when I read so many different inspirational books and longed for a different kind of life, I didn't realize that my life had already begun to turn around. In my studies and experiences since, I've observed that many people hope for a single lucky day when everything permanently changes for the better. It might be the moment that they finally discover their life's true calling, or meet their ideal mate, or finally get that big break. In reality, it's rarely that simple.

What I've discovered in my own journey is that changing your life from miserable—or just plain mundane—to marvelous requires a continually progressive, multi-layered process. I've learned a staggering number of lessons over the last ten years of intense personal growth, and bit by bit each lesson contributed to the creation of a much more satisfying, authentic life. This book is my attempt to share all that I've learned with you.

When I sat down and examined all the things I've learned that have gotten me from "there" to "here," I observed that I could divide them into seven different essential areas, which I present as the seven steps in this book. If you learn to pay careful attention to each of these in your life, and continually work on and grow in each area, I guarantee that you will dramatically improve your experience of happiness and health in your lifetime.

This book will now be part of your journey. Some chapters or points you'll get right away. Other sections you might resist or doubt. Keep your mind open, and let yourself entertain the possibility that a more rewarding experience of life might be within your reach.

I encourage you to buy yourself a beautiful bound book (or even just a simple wire-bound notebook) to write, reflect, and dream in as you travel through the pages of this book. Whenever I feel the winds of hope and change start to blow, I'll begin writing down my dreams and ideas for the next version of my life. As I write this, I'm entering one of those new life phases, and feel those winds swirling around me. Do you feel them, too?

I'd also like to give you a little gift, to thank you for being here with me: a free copy of the companion workbook for this book. To get your own complimentary copy of the downloadable workbook that I've created for you, go to www.susanbiali.com/workbook.html, right now, and download it so that you've got it ready to go, before you read another word.

The exercises in the workbook will give you the opportunity to reflect on how each chapter applies to you and your life, and will help you determine the most important steps you need to take next. You'll have a constructive way to take the "feel-good" inspirations and information that you receive from the pages of this book, and immediately apply them to yourself and your life. Doing this as you read through the book will help you transform your insights into real changes that you'll see and celebrate in your life.

I hope that this book blesses you, your life, and everyone around you. As you turn the pages, I hope that you'll begin to see the meaning and opportunity in your most difficult challenges, and that you'll simultaneously awaken the talents, dreams, and life that uniquely belong to you. More than anything, it's my dream that you'll learn to see life in a whole new way, a way that will make life feel better than it ever has before, no matter what's going on around you.

Here's to your very best life!

—Susan Biali, M.D.

1

ALLOW YOURSELF
TO BE
YOU

1

MY STORY

THE NIGHT FELT like it would never end. Fighting to keep my eyes open, I admitted one critically ill patient after another into the hospital's Cardiac Care Unit. As I went through the motions of examining patients, writing orders, and calling attending physicians, I prayed that the bulky "Code Blue" pager, which hung heavily from the waistband of my hospital greens, would never go off.

Whenever I could grab a few precious minutes, I retreated to my windowless cell and lay on the rough, antiseptic sheets of the small hard bed. Cold, uncomfortable, and totally miserable, I longed to sleep but couldn't, as a stream of footsteps and squeaking stretchers rushed down the hallway outside my door.

When I finally walked out of the sliding hospital doors, late in the afternoon the following day, it was already dark. Throughout my endless shift I'd dreamed of going home, yet when I finally opened my front door and dropped my bags on the floor, I came home to nothing.

I had nothing to look forward to, nothing to live for. No reason at all to go to bed and wake up the next morning. When I opened my eyes, I'd just go back for more of the same.

After finishing my Emergency Medicine residency and becoming an ER physician, I'd be able to work fewer hours. But the nature of the work, and the stress associated with it, would never change. Eleven years of university education, almost $100,000 in debt, and twenty-eight years of life behind me, and the only thing I had to show for it was a life that I dreaded waking up to every day.

I seemed to be the only one with a problem, as everyone else around me was absolutely thrilled. My whole life, I'd dedicated myself to making my parents, and all other grown-ups around me, proud by achieving high grades, awards, and scholarships. My becoming a doctor was the cherry on the sundae for them all. I'd be set for life. My parents would never have to worry about me, their oldest, eternally successful daughter. Or so they thought.

Though no one noticed, the cracks in my perfect mask had started to appear more than a decade earlier. In my teens, I struggled with an eating disorder, hating my body and myself. I counted calories and exercised obsessively with the goal of becoming perfectly (read: "model-thin") beautiful.

Halfway through my first year of med school, as I pushed myself towards my familiar position at the top of the class, I suddenly experienced several weeks of baffling, crippling panic attacks. Though the attacks eventually went away, things never quite went back to normal. By the time I graduated medical school and entered one of the most coveted residency programs in the country, the mild unhappiness that had shadowed my life for years had become a full-blown depression.

That night after my Cardiac Care Unit shift, I crumpled down onto my carpet, right next to where I'd thrown my bags. I remember sobbing endlessly, and my prayers for help quickly turned to thoughts of ending it all.

I didn't know how to do anything other than be a doctor. I couldn't think of any other way that I could survive in this world. How would I pay off my student loans? There was only one way out that I could see.

As I lay there, considering "exit" options, the phone rang. It was one of the senior Emergency Medicine residents, a woman who'd always been very kind to me.

"How are you?" she asked me. "I've noticed that you haven't quite seemed yourself lately. Is everything all right?"

An expert at faking perfection, I instantly slapped my mask right back on.

"I'm fine, thanks," I responded, cheerfully. "How are you?"

She didn't let me get away with it.

"The reason I'm calling, Susan, is because I want to talk to you about something. Do you remember hearing about the resident who took her life a few years ago?"

I did.

She went on. "Well, I thought it might be important for you to know that she took her life at the exact point in her residency where you are now, during her Cardiac Care Unit rotation." She paused to let that sink in, and then continued. "I'm going to ask you one more time. How are you, *really?*"

For the first time in twenty-eight years, my perfect mask fell off and shattered into a thousand pieces around me. I confessed everything: that I'd made a mistake choosing Emergency Medicine as a specialty, that I had had enough of the huge workload, and how the antidepressants had helped at first, but didn't seem to be working anymore.

She then said something that no one in my whole life had ever said to me.

"You know, Susan, you don't have to do this if you don't want to."

Never once had I considered that I, the long forgotten real me, the one who was crying her eyes out, might have a say in anything. I'd always let the overachieving, people-pleasing super me drive the bus. I'd ignored the real me for so long that I didn't even know who she was anymore. But I did know one thing: she wanted out.

The senior resident pointed out that I had enough credits to get my general license as a physician, and told me to go to my doctor and get an immediate stress leave. The power of her final sentence still rings in my head today: "Take some time off and think about what you really want to do with your life."

I WENT TO my doctor, and she gave me seven weeks stress leave, a gift so mind-boggling to an overworked, sleep-deprived resident that I could hardly believe it was happening. I still didn't know what I might really want to do with my life, and I wasn't sure that I'd ever find the courage to leave my residency, but I knew this: I was going to buy a ticket to Cuba.

Why Cuba? I can't explain it, other than I simply knew it. I didn't even know anyone who had gone there. But now, for some reason, I knew that it was time to go. And I had to go alone.

Whenever you get a clear impulse to do or try something different, especially when the idea seems to "come out of nowhere," it's usually something that will turn out to be immensely important to your life path. That is, if you're able to find the courage and faith to do it. The more crazy or improbable an idea seems, the greater its potential power to transform your life—in the very best of ways. Of course, the more unusual the idea, the more terrified and doubtful you'll feel as you consider it.

To make this sudden trip to Cuba feel less risky, I booked a week at an all-inclusive resort on Veradero Beach. When I got there and watched the other happy tourists gathered around the pool, I felt as if I'd suddenly woken up. I'd spent the last six years around medical students, residents, and doctors, and had somehow gotten the idea that it was normal to work around the clock, sleep in hospital greens, and focus my life on textbooks, facts, and diseases.

In Cuba, I was surrounded by people celebrating with their friends and families, who told me stories of other vacation adventures and the fun things they did at home. These people worked to live, they didn't live to work. And some of them even liked what they did!

I'd brought my journal with me, as a back-up in case I didn't make any friends and spent all my time alone. I didn't end up having much time to write, but in one entry I did find myself writing a very surprising sentence: "I want to be a writer."

I had no experience writing, and had avoided all arts-related courses in university. Writing essays would mean that my professors could grade me based on their whims or moods, something that was much too risky for my perfect GPA. And now, suddenly, I wanted to be a writer? It seemed bizarre, and totally out of character, but during that magical trip, anything seemed possible.

One night, after I'd finished my usual race through every dish on the buffet, I chose a seat in the theatre and waited for the evening's show to start. If I close my eyes right now, I can put myself right back in that chair, and can re-live every detail of what happened next.

The lights dimmed, and a spectacularly alive mix of horns, percussion, and piano music blared from the speakers. Then came the moment I'll never forget: a sensational team of Cuban salsa dancers exploded onto the stage. At that very moment, I remembered who I really was.

When I was eight years old, if you'd asked me what I wanted to be when I grew up, I would've told you, without hesitating. With great drama and poise, I would have said this: "*I* am going to be—a Solid Gold Dancer."

I'm a little embarrassed by this now, having recently watched some original clips of my dance "idols" on YouTube. I'm surprised my parents even let me watch the show, though in my innocence I didn't know what those scantily-clad women and their gyrations were really all about.

All I knew, when I was eight, was that one day I was going to be on stage, on TV, wearing glamorous costumes and blowing everyone's minds with my fabulous dance moves. I couldn't understand why my mom wouldn't sign me up for dance lessons. I know now that it was because she feared that being around perfect little girls in pink leotards would make me both neurotic and vain. Instead, she signed me up for "healthier" gymnastics classes. Unfortunately, she never anticipated that by the time I was ready to start competing, they would regularly weigh and measure me in front of the other girls, unfavorably comparing my natural healthy curves to the tiny bodies of the rest of the team.

Despite all this, I still somehow knew that I had to prepare for my certain future on the stage, so I created my own studio in the basement, complete with a record player, my collection of ABBA records, and a sliding glass door that I could watch my dancing reflection in. I danced every night, for hours on end, choreographing my own dances and copying dance poses that I found in encyclopedias and library books.

My parents didn't know what I was really doing downstairs, and a few years later it all came to an end. Around the time when I was ten, my teachers suddenly discovered that I was "gifted." From that day forward, life revolved around school, studying, and getting straight A's and as much praise from the adults around me as possible. I finally had their attention, and I decided that academic achievement, not dancing, must be my destiny.

Eighteen years passed. Other than an uninspiring jazz dance class that I took in high school and an award-winning stint on stage as a dancing, singing "Spice Nurse" in my med school Skits Night competition, I forgot that I was a dancer, destined for fame, fortune, and miles of glittery spandex. But on that night in Cuba, I remembered.

When I got home from my trip, I resigned from my residency, and signed up for my first salsa dance class. People thought it was cute, until they realized how serious I was. I sucked up my dance classes like a sponge, and practiced every night at home, dancing to a black-market salsa CD that I'd bought on my last day in Cuba.

I went out to local salsa clubs every night that I could, and I remember offending, and even getting into arguments with, friends who sometimes joined me for nights out dancing. The problem: I would joyfully, without hesitation, drop a conversation mid-sentence any time someone came along and swept me off onto the dance floor.

My friends didn't understand, because they went out dancing to socialize and to have fun. I was dancing for my life. And I found it.

Within months, I was performing on a professional dance team, and within a couple of years, my dance partner and I had our eyes on an international salsa competition in Los Angeles. For our qualifying performance, we chose a Spanish theme—he'd be a lonely, fast-footed sailor who'd just gotten off his ship in the Andalusian port of Cadiz. I was supposed to be a hot-blooded Spanish flamenco dancer who emerged, dancing, out of the shadows. We'd see each other across the dock, fall in love, and then dance together, ending the number with a whirlwind, flamenco-flavored salsa dance routine.

I wasn't about to try to imitate flamenco on an international stage, so I signed up for private classes. After one class with our local flamenco legend, Oscar Nieto, I stopped practicing salsa at home. Instead, I rehearsed my new flamenco moves, over and over again. I was head over heels in love.

Shortly after, I injured my back dancing at a salsa club, when an overenthusiastic Venezuelan threw me into a position that is appropriately called a "neck drop." My salsa dreams, for the moment, were over. Amazingly, I found that I didn't care, as my heart was already somewhere else. A few months later, I got on a plane to join a new flamenco-dancing friend in Spain, to study in "the cradle of flamenco," Jerez de la Frontera. Since I'd only just started dancing and barely knew the basics, my flamenco teachers told me that it was much too early to go. But again, just like that trip I took to Cuba, I knew that it was the right thing to do.

My teacher in Spain, who was famous for making even advanced students cry, commented repeatedly in class about how quickly I picked up the steps, and invited me and my friend to rent the little apartment on the main floor of her house. In her smoke-filled little dance studio, I gained a confidence in my dance abilities that I carry with me to this day.

In the midst of all this dancing, I worked as a doctor in walk-in clinics, gradually paying down my student loans. Though I like people, and love health and wellness, I didn't like my job, and found myself feeling increasingly isolated from other "normal" doctors.

Even working part-time, my tension and resentment would gradually build, until I could barely get through the intense, patient-filled days. The only things that relieved that tension were my nights out dancing and the vacation breaks that I took whenever I could. My trips gave me something to look forward to, and kept me going through those long clinic days that never ended quickly enough.

Whenever I worked in the clinic, I'd glance at my watch every few minutes, unable to believe how slowly time passed. When I was out dancing, the night went by so quickly that it felt like it was over before it really started.

I fantasized about living somewhere exotic and glamorous, like Spain or Italy, and sensed that my life and my man were out there somewhere. Every time I traveled, I hoped to finally find "my" life. Each uneventful trip left me frustrated and disappointed, but I refused to let go of the dream—and it refused to let go of me.

Those years, I was still trying hard to be someone I wasn't. I wanted to be happy as a practicing physician, help lots of people, and buy a big beautiful house, like the other doctors I knew. I know now that I simply wasn't allowed to be content with that work because it wasn't what I was meant to do in this world.

In my journal, I dreamed of other ways that I could make enough money to fund my life and travels. I fantasized about being a travel writer and photographer (a dream which eventually did come true), and about becoming a health writer for national magazines.

I studied books about becoming a writer, took courses, and read page after page of advice—which told me how likely I was to fail, and how hard it would be for me to get published. I don't know why so many people in this world seem to feel that it's their responsibility to tell you why you shouldn't try something, and why you're going to fail if you do. If you dream of doing something, go for it. In my opinion and experience, if you dream something, it's because you *can* do it, or you're supposed to gain something wonderful from the experience of trying. Don't ever let anyone, no matter how much of an "expert" they are, convince you not to try something that feels right to you.

The year that I decided to become a writer, I sent unsolicited article ideas to three national magazines. I ended up being published in all three, and one, *The Medical Post*, immediately offered me a monthly nutrition column, which I wrote for eight years.

I lead a charmed life simply because I make use of the talent, inspiration, and opportunities that God gives me. I know that's the source of the ideas in my head and heart, and my job is simply to take the chance and give them a try.

How many crazy or improbable ideas have you had that you've never tried because you were sure that the odds were against you? Or worse, because someone else told you that the odds were against you?

Within three years of quitting my residency, I was a professional freelance writer, was beginning to get invited to speak across the country, and was performing flamenco on Saturday nights with my favorite teacher of all time, Kasandra "La China," in our local flamenco café.

I still didn't like my day job, and still longed to find "my" country, and my man. By now, my friends and family were sick of hearing me complain about wanting to change my life. They encouraged me to learn to be grateful with things as they were. After all, how many people would have loved to have my "perfect" life? But as hard as I tried to be happy with things the way they were, I still had that longing in my heart that wouldn't let me go—an unshakeable feeling that things still weren't quite right. Not yet, at least.

That fall, I followed another impulse and booked a solo trip to Puerto Vallarta, Mexico. When I saw Armando leading a group dance by the side of the pool, I said "No!" to myself, out loud. I'd come to Mexico to reflect on my life and to write, and had no intention of having a holiday romance. My resolve lasted less than twenty-four hours.

Six weeks later, I visited Armando again, and shortly after that he visited me for three months in Canada. That November, I packed all the possessions that would fit into my trusty Honda, and he drove me across the continent to Puerto Vallarta.

It had taken me months to convince Armando that I wasn't out of my mind. After all, how could a young physician with a great income and career give it all up to dance, write, and live in a one-room cockroach-infested apartment in a Mexican beach town?

Today, he has learned to trust my "crazy" ideas. And despite his doubts, Armando, who is now my husband, has turned out to be the biggest supporter and cheerleader of my dance and life dreams. Thanks to him, I eventually moved to Cabo San Lucas on the Baja peninsula, where my dance dreams finally came true on a scale grander than I could ever have imagined. That's what happens when you give your dreams a chance and refuse to give up.

I went through years of struggle in Mexico to finally make my flamenco dreams a reality, enduring setback after setback. When I finally got my breakthrough, I could hardly believe the spectacular events that quickly followed. I had just wanted a stage to perform on and an audience to dance for; I never thought that I'd end up dancing for and teaching celebrities, in some of the most beautiful hotels and private villas in the world. "Don't give up before the miracle," as the old twelve-step saying goes.

By following my heart and paying attention to signposts along the way (which came along in the form of crises, mental illness, physical illness, people, and flashes of inspiration, to name just a few), my life has turned into something so wonderful that I couldn't possibly have invented it myself.

Today, I use these experiences to help people improve the quality of their lives, in a way so much bigger than when I just used to hand them prescriptions to treat their coughs. Stories like mine are possible when, step by step, you listen to your heart and create a life that's true to the real you.

There's so much more to my story than I've been able to fit into these pages, and I'll share more details with you as we go along. The reason I thought it was important to open this book this way is that I wanted to illustrate what happens when you honor your true self, no matter what anyone else has to say about it. The ironic thing is that the people who are most opposed to your ideas when you first start out are often the ones who cheer the loudest for you at the end.

This isn't about creating a self-indulgent "me, me, me" kind of life. Rather, it's about finally having the courage to recognize the person who you really are, and to make your most important life choices based on that.

Your most authentic life, and your biggest contribution to society, come from the wonderful tapestry made up of all the parts of you—your flaws, your mistakes, your dreams, your talents, your experiences, and your natural likes and dislikes. You are completely unique on this planet and in history, and you are here for a reason. Until you start being the real you, in all areas of your life, you can't possibly experience the fullness of the life that most certainly is waiting for you.

My days used to feel like a life sentence. Luckily I don't always believe what people tell me, otherwise I would possibly have accepted the "reality" that I was a biologically depressed person who would have to stay on anti-depressants for most of her life. Today, I can't remember when I popped my last "happy pill."

From the moment that I remembered who I really am, and gave myself permission to be my true self, I began making choices that were right for me, instead of listening to what other people thought would be best. And that's when everything began to turn around, and the darkness turned to light. People used to feel sorry for me. Today, they tell me that they envy my fulfillment and freedom.

Now, I'm going to share my secrets with you. You, too, can enjoy a life full of miracles and meaning, no matter who you are and where you are right now. So let's get started!

2

WHO ARE YOU, REALLY?

*W*HO WOULD YOU be if anything was possible? When I ask you that, what's the first thought that comes to your mind? Do you instantly dismiss that thought as being crazy or impractical?

Do you think that becoming your most authentic, ideal self would be too selfish? Would it be unfair to everyone around you to suddenly decide to become someone else, even if that "someone else" is actually the real you? Do you worry that by becoming the real you, you might lose everything in your life that feels comfortable, secure, and familiar?

It's natural to feel most comfortable when you're doing, and being, what's normal to everyone around you. Human beings are socialized, and perhaps even programmed, to go along with what's average. It's also natural that when you start making original, unexpected choices, it will feel strange at first, and some people around you will start to feel uncomfortable, or even scared.

When I was a "well-behaved," academically successful physician with traditional goals, everyone around me felt safe and assured, content with my choices in life. When I started to rebel against the status quo, to save my own life, everyone seemed to have an opinion. Some people criticized me, other people ridiculed me, and some of the people closest to me became downright angry about what I was doing. Even strangers felt that they had the right to accuse me of being selfish, when they had only known me for all of five minutes. This usually happened as soon as I mentioned that I used to be a full-time doctor, but had decided to focus on writing and dancing instead.

I wouldn't bother telling them that traditional medical work made me feel depressed and unfulfilled. Experience had taught me that there wasn't (and isn't) much use in trying to win those people over. I could usually tell from their tone that they'd continue to insist that I had a duty to fulfill to the public, even if it ruined my own life. Besides, if I couldn't hack it as a doctor, there must be something wrong with me, right?

The one thing I have learned to say to such people is this: "I found that it wasn't enough to just help one person at a time. I want to help millions of people improve their quality of life and health. I can't do that in a medical office, but I *can* do that through writing, speaking and working with the media." Few people would ever agree with me, but I know it to be true. And that's good enough for me.

Even you might not see how dancing fits into my goal of "helping lots of people," but it does. My unusual life story makes me different from other doctors, which gets me attention from the media. I then use these opportunities to teach as many people as I can about principles of life and health. I didn't anticipate that result when I started dancing; I thought I was dancing just for me, and no one else.

YOUR HEART HOLDS THE BLUEPRINT
FOR YOUR BEST LIFE

When you honor yourself, you'll get all kinds of wonderful, unanticipated results that will lead you into your best life. The blueprints for that life can be found in the hopes, dreams, passions, and talents that make up the real you.

Honoring your passions and being yourself will help you meet your other goals in life in ways that you have never imagined. I'm telling you, it's just the most amazing phenomenon!

That's why I chose to begin this book by emphasizing how important it is to start being the real you, no matter how impractical that might seem. There will never be another you. If you spend your life denying that real you, and focus on being like everyone else, that unique you, who is meant to be here, who *is* here, will never make it out into the daylight. And whatever it is that you were supposed to do, or experience, will die with you. I believe that you need to honor every wonderful, silly, "inappropriate" part of you, because your unique personality contains the roadmap for your best life.

After quitting my Emergency Medicine residency, I could have just been a doctor. I wouldn't have been very passionate about my life, but I would have had lots of financial security, and everyone around me would have approved of my choice. I'm a pretty good doctor, and I care about people, so I probably would have done a reasonable amount of good in this world. At the end, I would have known that I'd lived a good, decent life, and that I'd made a contribution.

But I wouldn't have done what I truly came here for. I wouldn't have fulfilled my personal destiny. If I'd decided to ignore who I really was inside, and had chosen the practical and comfortable route instead, you wouldn't be reading this book. All the people who read my newsletter, and tell me that something I wrote changed their lives, wouldn't have experienced those benefits. The people who hear me speak on the radio, see me on TV, and email me to tell me that my words came at the perfect moment in their life wouldn't have heard those words.

If you choose to neglect the real you, what will the world miss out on? If you can't think of anything right now, it doesn't mean that you don't have anything to contribute. Most likely, you just need to allow yourself more time and space to connect with the real you.

I have my moments of doubt, too. Sometimes I wonder if what I'm doing and teaching really is valuable. I ask myself: "Will my words really help people? Am I just being selfish? Am I misguidedly encouraging others to be selfish?"

But then I give a speaking presentation and people come up to me afterward to hug me and thank me with tears streaming down their faces. I watch my coaching clients experience miracle after miracle, simply by making choices that honor themselves. That's why I keep doing this, and that's why I'm writing these words to you, right now.

DETACH AND BE YOU

When was the last time that you truly detached from everything around you and gave yourself a chance to just *be*? One of the best ways to do this is to physically remove yourself from the activities and places associated with your usual daily routines and do something different. You don't have to go far to find yourself, and it's cheap and easy to explore your own local surroundings.

Think about where in your city or local area you might be able to go. The ideal place gives you opportunities to both wander and to sit and reflect. It might be an art gallery that you've always wanted to visit or a hiking path that leads to a wonderful look-out. Is there an inviting street in your town that you could stroll along, with restaurants or coffee shops that you've never visited?

You could also take a long drive—no music, no radio, just your own thoughts for company. Whether you can get away for an hour or an entire day, do whatever you can. If your life or schedule prevents you from easily leaving the house or your workplace, pour yourself a cup of tea or coffee and pull a chair up to a window. Sit there, watch the view, and let your mind take you where it wants you to go. Take time to give yourself the necessary peace and space.

I remember one beautiful snowy day, six years ago. That morning, I got into my car and drove north for two hours to pick up some information from a person who lived close to the Whistler ski resort area. When I left the meeting, I impulsively decided to drive the rest of the way to the resort, and pulled into the parking lot opposite the beautiful Fairmont Chateau Whistler.

As I wandered through the lobby into the hotel's cozy mountainside lounge, my eyes inhaled the views of snow-capped pines and tall mountains that filled the towering windows. I found a seat in front of a roaring fire, ordered a steaming hot chocolate, and took my journal out of my bag. Out of nowhere, I suddenly found myself writing about how, one day, I'd move to Mexico.

I jotted down financial figures, plans, and creative ideas as to how I might be able to pull it off. At the time, I doubted that I could ever make it happen, but I started to feel that tingling of possibility, a glimmer of childlike hope.

Though I'd been dancing salsa for a couple of years at that point, I hadn't even the slightest idea that one day I would earn income as a professional flamenco dancer in Los Cabos. Nor did I imagine that I would meet and marry a Mexican and commute between Mexico and Vancouver for four years, spending blissful weeks and even months soaking up the sun between trips to the north.

That day, in front of that cozy fire, I simply conceived the dream. At the time it felt like too much to ask for, but there it was, on the page.

When you take the time to get away from all the noise of daily life, and get quiet enough to let yourself feel what the real you really cares about, dreams of, and longs for, you open yourself to the experiences and life that are waiting for you. The more often you're able to step out of your usual routine and connect with that essential, authentic you, the more fuel you'll feel behind you as you take your first steps toward a more authentic life. The wonderful things that will happen as a result are simply part of the natural, meant-to-be life that unfolds when you listen to your true self.

DOCTORS, DANCERS, POETS, AND QUEENS

If you're still stuck and unsure about who you really are, close your eyes and remember who you were when you were around eight or nine years old. At that age, you were old enough to have an awareness of yourself and the huge buffet of options offered by the world around you, yet you were still young enough that the adults around you probably hadn't gotten serious about your future—yet.

Whenever I give a lecture, I usually give the audience the opportunity to ask me questions. Public speaking terrifies most people, so I'm often faced with a roomful of wide-eyed, close-mouthed faces. When this happens, I try to get things going myself, by walking up to someone and asking them, *"When you were a child, what did you want to be when you grew up?"*

Then the fun really starts. Once that person answers, everyone else starts chiming in. I've heard all kinds of wonderful things, everything from "I wanted to be a poet" to "I wanted to be a policewoman" to "I saved up all my quarters and then personally called the creator of the musical *Annie* to tell him he needed to cast me in the lead role" (that's a true story).

Probably the most common answer I hear is "I wanted to be a singer." The other day at a conference, an audience member said that she had always wanted to be a singer, and that when she was a little girl she used to sing herself to sleep at night—at full volume! One night, her father knocked on her bedroom door and asked her to stop singing, because the noise was keeping her brother awake.

"I still dream of singing, and I would love to perform," she told us, "but I never got over that memory of my father telling me to be quiet. I didn't realize until now that that's why I feel like I can't sing in front of anyone—that's what has been holding me back all these years." I'm pretty sure that nothing's holding her back now.

Once I get people talking about their distant childhood dreams, I probe further, asking them if they ever fulfilled this vision for their life. If they didn't, I ask them when the last time was that they wrote a poem or sang a song. Usually it was long ago. "It's too late," or "I'm too old now," they'll almost always tell me. What's your excuse?

Listen to me now: You are *never* too old. Never. Someone just emailed me a video of an eighty-seven-year-old woman dancing salsa better than I ever did at my peak, in my twenties. There's always some small way that you can incorporate some aspect of that childhood dream into your life, right now.

Rent a favorite childhood movie, play a sport you haven't played since you were ten, go through old photo albums and reminisce about the things you loved to dream and do. Amazing things will happen if you just take one step, and then another, towards that child, that fabulous limitless you who used to dream such wonderful dreams.

I know a successful comic who had wanted to be a comedian, ever since he was a little boy. For years, he never even tried it, because it seemed so silly and impractical. He worked at a conventional job and became more and more depressed until, one day, things got so bad that he decided that he had nothing to lose anymore. He summoned up all the courage he possessed and told his wife that he was going to give this comedy thing a try. Soon after, he got his first local comedy club appearance.

His only intention, at the time, was to finally honor this thing that he'd always wanted to do. Even if he only did it once, he could at least put his heart to rest, knowing that he'd given himself and that little boy in his heart a chance.

He admits that his first performance was terrible, but the owners of the club still saw something in him. He gave one performance after another, moving to more and more prestigious venues, and today he's not only a full-fledged, award-winning stand-up comedian, but also a popular TV and radio host. He loves his life, and so does his wife. All this because of the vision he had for his life when he was a child—an "impractical" vision that turned out to hold his most fulfilling, wonderful adult future inside.

I mentioned earlier that when I was a little girl I dreamed of being a glitzy Solid Gold Dancer. I also wanted to be a journalist and write books. I especially loved to put a crown on my head, sit on my "throne" in my living room, and dispense wisdom to the invisible members of my imaginary kingdom. When I discovered that it made more practical sense to excel at math and science, I shoved that visionary little leader into the darkest recesses of my heart, and started on the path that eventually led to becoming a doctor. Thankfully, that little girl refused to die, and she rocketed back into my life as soon as I gave her the opportunity.

I'm not a Solid Gold Dancer (thank goodness!), but I still get to dance on stage, and occasionally on TV, in fabulous costumes. As a freelance writer and published photographer, I have fulfilled my dream of becoming a journalist. What's more, this is the first of the books that I dreamed of writing. As for being a queen, I don't get to wear a jeweled crown as often as I'd like to, but I do get to share what passes for wisdom with a lot of wonderful audiences.

Who were you as a little child? What did you love to do? What made you jump up and down for joy? What wonderful, grand plans did you have for your life? That marvelous little powerhouse of energy and creativity that you used to be may well hold the keys to your most fulfilling version of you today.

WHO ARE YOU BECOMING TODAY?

When I ask you to reflect on who you really are, I'm not just referring to the authentic, long-lost you that may be hiding under the familiar layers of your everyday self and life. I'd also like you to think about who you are today, and who you are becoming.

If you don't decide to take charge of who you're going to be in this life, your life will decide it for you. Do you know what's influencing you right now, and what's setting the course for the rest of your life?

We often don't think of the things we do day-to-day or the influences that we let into our life. They may seem innocent on their own, but over time they really add up.

What do you allow—even put—into your mind? Who do you let into your life? What's going on around you? What could be the long-term result?

I read a lot, and I have discovered that what I choose to read can have a huge effect on my life. Years ago, I used to read novels that featured outrageously rich characters, lots of drama, and plenty of sordid affairs and betrayals. Guess what my life was like?

I wasn't rich, but I did spend a lot of money that I didn't have. My romantic life was a mess, and my friends loved calling me a "drama queen."

I love the work of business and life philosopher Jim Rohn, and he's always talking about the importance of reading. According to Rohn, the books you read today are turning you into the person you'll be tomorrow. Take a look at your bookshelf or your bedside table. How do you like the future you?

Now, when you think about the kind of person you'd like to be in ten years, what kind of books would help get you there? Do you wish you could develop more spiritual faith, or self-confidence, or knowledge in a certain area? Choose someone you know who you admire, who's living a life that you'd like to live one day, and ask them what their favorite books are.

Who do you spend the most time with? Like it or not, you're becoming more like them. When you consider the people around you every day, is the fact that you're becoming more like them a good thing or a bad thing?

They say that your income tends to be the average of the incomes of the five people that you spend the most time with. I'd expect that the same rule would hold true for all kinds of personal qualities: kindness, generosity, spirituality, success, and so on.

As an example, I've gone through various degrees of polite and impolite language throughout my life. When I was a little girl, I read a lot and loved to use big words. Unfortunately, this didn't go over well on the playground. I quickly tired of being made fun of for my "prissy, goody-two-shoes" way of talking and, to my mother's horror, quickly recovered my reputation by peppering my language with every obscenity known to man (that is, every obscenity known to ten-year-olds in the early '80s).

I'm embarrassed to say that it probably wasn't until I was in my mid-twenties that I finally had the self-confidence to start cleaning up my language, and it was pretty squeaky clean by the time I became a doctor. Until one day last year.

I went to a friend's birthday party and ran into a fun acquaintance whom I'd met a couple of times before. My husband and I chatted with her for a while, exchanging amused glances as she came up with phrase after phrase that would put a sailor to shame.

The next day, my husband and I were laughing and talking about something, and I was shocked by the words that came out of my mouth. A few hours later, there they were again. I wasn't anywhere near my acquaintence's level of self-expression, but these were phrases that hadn't left my lips in years, plus some new ones. It astounded me how contagious her language had proven to be, after just half an hour of conversation.

What are the things that the people around you talk about most? Money? Gloom and doom? Or worse yet, do they spend all their time criticizing and gossiping about others?

Living between Canada and Mexico, I noticed a dinner-table phenomenon. When I dined with friends in Mexico, we talked about local happenings, caught up on each other's lives, and exchanged funny stories. By comparison, mealtime conversation with friends and family in Canada seemed to always turn to the price of real estate, personal incomes, investments and other money-related topics. Even the cab drivers would talk about money as they drove me to the airport! After a week or two in Canada, I'd start thinking that I needed to work more, generate more income, and buy a house as soon as possible. Luckily, that would wear off once I was back in Mexico for a few days.

I choose my friends carefully. I try my best to love all people, but I try to limit the amount of time that I spend in the presence of the ones that I know influence me in negative ways.

Thanks to my spiritual beliefs and experiences, I now enjoy a sense of peace that I had never imagined possible. Sure, I still have moments of worry or fear, but these are far less frequent than they once were.

In contrast, a few dear friends of mine have the unfortunate habit of seeing the potential for disaster everywhere they turn. Mention an idea to them, and they'll tell you what could and will go wrong. If they share a story from their lives, they'll focus on all the terrible things that happened, because in their minds life is just so unfair. What scares me most about talking to people like this is that they often point out potential problems or disasters that I didn't even know existed!

The way that I live my life and make my choices relies so much on faith, optimism, and belief in everything working out for the best. The worldview of these negative people could threaten my future if I let their fears take hold in my mind. The same goes for people who tell me that my ideas are ridiculous or will only lead to the poorhouse. I run away from those people without looking back.

It's important to love people, but it's also important to guard your own mental, emotional and spiritual well-being, especially if another person's way of seeing the world, or you, could prevent you from making the contribution to the world that you were meant to make.

Every day we make choices. We choose the food that we put into our bodies, the shows that we watch on TV, the things we read, and the people we spend time with. The next time you start to automatically do any of these things, stop and think about the effect that it will have on you. How will it contribute to the "you" of the future? Does it fit with your vision for you and your life?

The very best part of this is that now that you're aware of all the things that are influencing you, you can begin to make conscious choices that will shape both you and your life. Choose good influences, and you will virtually guarantee yourself a meaningful, fulfilling life that you can enjoy and take pride in.

2

LEARN TO LOVE
YOURSELF

3

SELF-LOVE 101
(A MANDATORY COURSE)

I ONCE HAD A friend who drove me bananas. Every time I called her to complain about my life, or started moaning to her about what the latest guy was putting me through, she would sigh and calmly say: "Susan, in order for your life to change, you're first going to have to learn to love yourself."

I was convinced that she didn't know what she was talking about, and I resented her inability to help me in the way that I needed it most. I needed her to listen to me, to agree compassionately with all of my complaints, and to agree that she, too, didn't understand why bad things kept happening to good people like me.

On top of that, I couldn't actually understand what she meant by this vague "love yourself" thing, and I didn't know what I was supposed to do. I kept trying different things: vacations, shopping, several pieces of cake (eaten in one sitting), even a new relationship. They each felt good temporarily, but I'd always feel frustrated and unfulfilled afterwards. Because I didn't know what the real problem was, I'd go back again and again for more of these feel-good treats, though they seemed to help me less each time. I didn't have a clue as to how to effectively take care of myself, and yet I had tried everything that I could think of.

For a long time I didn't understand what my problem was and I felt very alone. Now, I know that there are plenty of people out there who feel the same, and I also know enough about real happiness and fulfillment to be able to coach others towards these goals.

Brian is a bachelor who asked me for help because he just couldn't get on track with his life. He felt like he was going in circles and couldn't get off the merry-go-round created by his long list of compulsive behaviors. One week he'd manage to kick his habit of drinking several beers by himself every night, but then the next week he'd park himself in front of the TV every night, eating entire bags of chips. I'd help him tidy up his neglected finances, and then he'd somehow manage to cover his desk with paralyzing clutter overnight. Once he'd sorted that out, he'd find himself on the Internet for hours, surfing and chatting on dating websites.

For a long time, he'd thought that these were just bad habits, things that he enjoyed that he simply had a hard time resisting. He didn't realize that his compulsive avoidance of himself, through each of these activities, was the real problem.

The more time Brian wasted losing himself in beer, food, financial chaos, or the Internet, the further he got from his true goals and purpose in life, and the worse he felt. The worse he felt, the more he felt he needed to lean on his destructive behavioral "crutches." Later, when he had to face the hangover, or his creditors, or the bathroom scale, his mood would take another spiral downwards. The day that he finally saw and accepted his addictive behaviors for what they truly were, his life began to turn around, and he began to move forward.

Do you have destructive, distracting patterns in your life that you keep repeating, patterns that keep you from fulfilling your goals? Perhaps you sabotage your weight by snacking on junk food. Perhaps you say that you want to be financially stable, but keep spending too much, or forget to pay your bills. Perhaps you claim to want a healthy, loving romantic relationship, but keep ending up in abusive or drama-filled situations. Perhaps you say you want more free time to spend with your family, but just can't seem to stop working, or 'net-surfing.

When you practice your type of "addictive" behavior, what is it doing for you? Does it make you feel better in the moment? Does it help you ignore something that you'd really rather not face? Does it give you an excuse for why you're not doing what you really should be doing with your time and your life? Does it keep you stuck in a frustrating but safe place that you really don't like very much but at least are familiar with?

As long as you automatically indulge in the behavior that temporarily makes you feel better or distracts you from your life, you probably aren't really aware of why you're doing it. You just know that something inside you wants to, and the urge seems almost impossible to control or stop.

Awareness is the antidote to addiction. Once you stop and ask yourself what it's really about, once you see your behavior for what it is and admit the full effect that it's having on your life, it'll never derail you in the same way again. This isn't something that's easy to do on your own, but thankfully there are lots of resources out there that can help you, depending on what kind of behavior you're stuck in.

Whether you betray yourself and your well-being through food, alcohol, drugs, over-spending, financial chaos, sex, or abusive relationships, there are many other people who've been right where you are, and who have successfully recovered themselves and their lives. Focused groups can be the most supportive, healing environments—look for online groups and discussion boards and search for meetings close to where you live. Look for experts and coaches who specialize in helping people get through the specific challenges you struggle with. Find books on the subject in the library.

(Note: Some people who aren't alcoholics but who struggle with other addictive types of behavior have found it extremely helpful to read the "Big Book" of Alcoholics Anonymous; if alcohol isn't your challenge, substitute in another relevant word—such as drugs, food, debt, sex, etc.—anywhere where the word "alcohol" is used. An online version of the AA Big Book can be found at www.aa.org/bigbookonline)

In my experience, each of these types of resources will help lead you back to the most important thing of all: your true self and your real life. That's where the real love and healing will begin. In my case, I also learned to turn to God—referred to in the twelve-step groups as our "higher power"—to help me with the areas of life that I couldn't seem to improve on my own.

I've observed that when people finally understand and release compulsive, escape-focused behavior, and finally see themselves for who they truly are, they naturally begin to follow the path leading to what they were truly meant to do here on this earth. That cleansing and reconnecting with your purest self is one of the greatest acts of self-love that you can do.

To help you understand this from another perspective, I'd like to talk about some of the ways in which many of us, without realizing it, regularly sabotage ourselves by using misguided definitions of "self-love."

DO YOUR "REWARDS" HELP OR HARM YOU?

I'm all for giving yourself treats and gifts—as long as they're usually carefully selected rewards that truly benefit you and your life.

It sounds simple, but it's actually a huge concept shift for most people. Think about it: what do you normally give to yourself as a "treat" or reward?

Do you battle with your weight and self-image because of a weakness for sweets or junk food? I struggle with it constantly, and can't keep sweet foods in the house—I'd be finding excuses to reward myself all day. ("I just wrote a paragraph! Time for a treat!") To prove my point, Armando brought home a box of cookies a couple of days ago because my parents were coming over for tea. My parents didn't end up coming over, which turned out to be a good thing, because the cookies are long gone. Armando only had one.

If sugary foods aren't your thing, maybe you treat yourself by going for a binge at the mall with your credit card—even though you can't really afford to. Or perhaps you celebrate a success or special occasion by going out for an all-night martini marathon, which not only empties your wallet but leaves you with a hangover for the rest of the weekend.

The tradition of rewarding ourselves or celebrating with sweets, spending, or alcohol is so deeply embedded into our culture that most of us choose them automatically, without actually reflecting on the impact that these choices have on us and our lives. Of course, in the moment they feel really good, too.

The next time you want to celebrate or treat yourself, ask yourself this: Is what you're about to do really consistent with what you want for yourself and your life? Will you feel happy afterwards, or guilty? What are some ways that you can reward yourself that you can still really look forward to, without feeling bad about it after?

Though I'm a very lazy cook, I love eating, and one of my favorite ways to reward myself at the end of a productive or successful day is to go out for dinner. I know how to make healthy choices from almost any menu, so the quality of the food isn't the problem. The problem is my credit card balance at the end of the month. I don't even want to think about how much money I've spent on restaurants in the last few years.

Armando and I have found two solutions to this problem, as we'd still like to be able to treat ourselves regularly to good food. The first solution is that we've found a couple of extremely inexpensive, family-run restaurants that serve healthy delicious food at a great price, so when we want to treat ourselves to a restaurant meal, we go there.

The second solution is that instead of going to a restaurant, we go to the supermarket around the corner and find some inexpensive, delicious ingredients to put together a special meal at home. We get a great movie (or find one on TV), spread out our "fancy" meal on the coffee table in front of the sofa, and ooh and aah over our fabulous homemade "restaurant" food. We've come up with so many great dishes (thanks to Armando's genius in the kitchen) that we're not nearly as tempted anymore to go out for food.

How do you like to reward yourself? Do you love to buy yourself a new outfit, but can't really afford it? Instead try going to a nice consignment store—I've found the most beautiful designer clothes in places like these, sometimes for under $10!

Do you like to treat yourself with sweet snack foods when you've had a tough day? Try something sweet and delicious but healthy, like a bowl of blueberries and raspberries topped with a big dollop of vanilla yogurt. Buy yourself one gourmet cookie, instead of an entire bag, and savor each delicious bite with your eyes closed.

Another guilt-free way to be good to yourself is to treat yourself to wonderful experiences that you really enjoy. Go to a restaurant with a gorgeous view and watch the sunset——but order only one glass of wine instead of an entire meal. Spend a whole day being a tourist in your own town. Sign yourself up for that course you've always meant to take. Go to the library and get that book you've always wanted to read, and then curl up in a cozy chair and read it. Think of all the ways you normally reward yourself (and often regret later), and come up with new versions that still feel good but support your financial, physical, or emotional well-being.

Choosing rewards wisely, as an act of self-love, doesn't mean living a life of boredom; you just need to get creative about finding rewards for yourself that actually contribute to—rather than damage—your health, life, and success.

That said, there's room in life for everything—a cookie here, a martini there—but I think you'll find that the more healthy, truly positive treats you create for yourself, the less you'll find yourself needing, or even enjoying, those old rewards.

MIRROR, MIRROR:
REFLECTIONS OF LOVE FOR YOURSELF

What do you see when you look in the mirror? Do you like what you see? If you're at home and you catch a glimpse of yourself in the hall or bedroom mirror as you go about your day, who do you see looking back at you? Have you taken some time to take care of your appearance, or did you just automatically throw on any old thing?

The amount of care that you take in your appearance is a measure of how much you care for yourself. It's also directly related to the way that you feel every time you pass a mirror, as you go about your day. How do you feel about how you look at this very moment?

This isn't about being excessively superficial or high-maintenance; it's about basic self-care and self-love. It makes me feel bad to catch my reflection whenever I haven't taken the time to pay proper attention to myself. When I take the time to get properly dressed and put on a little makeup, even if no one will see me all day, it's amazing how much better I feel about myself and my day. I might even smile at myself whenever I wash my hands in the bathroom sink.

Do you take care of yourself differently based on whether someone else will see you or not? Do you dress differently, depending on who you think might see you? I think almost everyone does this. You forget, or ignore, the fact that even if you don't go out all day and no one else is home, there is one person who will see you, the most important person of all—you!

By the way, this doesn't just apply to people who occasionally or frequently spend time on their own at home. It also applies to any time or any situation when you think that it's just not worth taking the time to properly attend to yourself. I used to just throw on a baseball hat and mismatched sweats to go grocery shopping, without even taking the time to brush my hair, until the day that I ran into one of my most important corporate clients at the store. Luckily he still hired me, but I never went out looking like that again!

If you've been feeling down, or sorry for yourself, or just plain blah about your life, take the time to put on something that you like in the morning (it doesn't need to be fancy, but ideally it should be something that you both feel and look good in), and do something, however basic, to take care of your face and hair. Take time for an invigorating hot shower. Shave what needs to be shaved, even if no one will see it. The times in your life when you least feel like making the effort are the times when it's most important and beneficial to do this.

CLEAR OUT THE CLUTTER

One of the most common ways that people block their lives, and block themselves from attending to their true needs, is through clutter. Clutter comes in many forms, not just the physical, and can represent several areas of your life: elements of the past that you need to let go of, useless aspects of the present that get in your way, and general chaos (often denied or avoided) that keeps you from moving ahead in the direction that you know you'd like to go.

Clutter can even represent fear. As long as it's there, bogging you down, you don't have to deal with the discomfort of moving forward into unfamiliar territory. It's much easier, and safer, to flounder around in the mess, pushing it from one corner of the room to the other, perhaps covering it up with a pretty cloth and flowers, hoping no one will notice. But you know it's there. It's an act of self-love to finally truly see that clutter, admit that it's holding you back, and decide to do something about it.

Almost every single one of my coaching clients has, at some point, complained to me about the amount of clutter in their life and home, and they'll often use it as an excuse for why they can't move forward. For example, someone may have a wonderful new business idea, but when I encourage her to begin working on it, she'll say:

"Oh, I wish I could, I'd love to, but I'd first have to make space for a new office in my house. I could use the spare room, but first I'll have to go through all the boxes and old papers I've got in there right now. Unless I get them out of the way, I won't have any room for a desk, so I can't get started. I really can't start my new business until I've gone through every single paper in that room."

It sounds logical, but when I try to get my box-blocked clients to set the goal of going through those boxes, even just spending half an hour a day, or an hour on the weekend, you wouldn't believe the excuses they come up with. They can't this week, they just don't have time, or (by the next session) they just didn't get around to it. Of course, they still found plenty of time to watch TV, to hang out with friends, to go the store to buy those snack foods that they wish they could stop eating.

I adore my coaching clients, so I'm not writing this to complain about them. I can be just as guilty of this behavior as they are. In most cases what we don't realize is that as much as we say that we hate the clutter, no matter how much it drives us crazy every time we see it, we're attached to it. It's safe.

As long as it's there, we don't have to buy that new desk, and don't have to start working on that new business idea. We can hold on to the dream, and even tell lots of other people about it, but as long as those boxes are in there, blocking things up, we don't need to risk failing, and we don't have to experience the changes in our lives that might come with success.

I noted earlier that the clutter I'm referring to isn't just the physical kind that most of us have in our desks and our homes. In addition to those boxes of old papers, piles of unused junk, and stacks of old magazines, our lives can get cluttered in more subtle ways. This clutter may not be obvious to our eyes, but it still drains us of our most precious resources: time, energy, and peace of mind.

What does your appointment schedule for the next few weeks look like? Is it filled with activities and people that you care about, that are in line with your most important values or goals? Or is it filled up with unnecessary, time-wasting clutter?

Who are the people you spend most of your time with? Do they contribute something meaningful and positive to your life, or do they add stress and negativity? Do you feel obliged to send hundreds of Christmas cards to people you haven't heard from, or laughed with, in years?

What about your work life? Are there unnecessary things that you are stuck doing that prevent you from meeting your professional goals? Do you need to organize your desk or your files? Are you aware of which of your various activities produces the most desired results? Do you plan your week, month, and year consciously or do you just plow through whatever comes your way, putting out fires as they appear and trying to survive?

Clutter, by nature, is overwhelming. Most likely, your natural response to clutter is to want to avoid it and run away. That strategy might work for the moment, but it only makes you feel worse the next time you are reminded of it. Here are some tips that can help you begin to de-clutter your life in a manageable, constructive way:

> *Start with what bothers or blocks you the most*

After reading this section of the book, you might be feeling more overwhelmed than ever. Perhaps you knew that your desk needed serious organizing, but hadn't realized that the emotional and financial areas of your life were also in a state of chaos and clutter.

When I work with clients on de-cluttering, I have them first address the area that's causing them the most frequent hassles or the greatest amount of pain.

For example, one client complained to me that for years her bathroom counter had been so jammed with creams and powders and makeup that she couldn't even see her countertop. She also had boxes of office documents she needed to organize, and closets stuffed with clothes she never wore, but the bathroom mess was something she had to look at multiple times every day, and it was driving her nuts.

In half an hour, she sorted through it all, saving the creams and makeup she actually used and throwing away everything old and expired. She took the old makeup that she never used and put it into gift bags for her young nieces (who were sure to be delighted with them).

Another area I often encourage clients to target first, if necessary, is their finances. Having a messy basement isn't likely to affect your ability to survive, but failing to pay bills or bouncing checks can get you into serious trouble. I'll write more about this in the following section.

❧ *De-clutter in small chunks or time periods*

One of my clients failed every time on her "de-cluttering homework," until we discovered the secret to her success. If her assignment was to "go through and organize" her storage locker, she wouldn't do it. In fact, she wouldn't even start. However, if we changed the wording of her assignment to "sort through and organize the storage locker for half an hour this weekend," she got it done. Even better, the half hour often turned into several productive hours.

Often an area of clutter seems so big that you don't even know where to start, and can't imagine ever finishing it once you do start. By breaking down the task into small manageable chunks and simply doing *something*, you'll find you gain an amazing amount of momentum and a very satisfying feeling of accomplishment.

❧ *Set yourself up so that the clutter won't return*

If you're like me, you'll spend an afternoon cleaning up your desk, only to have it looking just as bad, or worse, by the following day. Rather than spending your life continually cleaning up organizational, financial, or emotional messes, try to understand how things got so cluttered, and what you can do to prevent it happening in the future.

To resolve my desk issues, I recently bought a new desk that has lots of different built-in shelves for organizing books, documents, and files. Now that almost everything has its place, a lot less paper makes it onto the writing surface of my desk. I can also find things when I need them, which has greatly reduced my stress.

I also have stopped saying yes to every social invitation I receive, to keep my life from feeling like a hamster wheel that I can't get off. It helped to learn to use a digital planner which lets me see both my month and week at one glance, as that prevents me from double-booking or over-booking my life.

Once you open your eyes to the various forms of clutter in your life and start to peel it away, layer by layer, you'll be amazed at how much less stressed you will feel. Even more important, you'll finally be able to devote time to the things that really matter. Clearing the clutter enables you to spend time on the people and pursuits that fulfill you the most, and also clears the path to your dreams.

MIND YOUR MONEY

Money deserves a special mention in this book, as it's one of the ways in which we abandon ourselves most frequently. The way you handle money can dramatically affect your experience of life, the amount of stress you live with day-to-day, and your very ability to survive.

What does your financial life look like? Are your finances cluttered (think unfiled or unorganized documents, unopened bills, and too many credit cards)? Are they hopelessly disorganized? Do you know where your money goes?

I have another question for you: How much time did you spend planning your last major vacation? If you're like me, you probably researched several different destinations, checked out different guidebooks and looked at hotels online (reading online reviews and looking through their photo albums), and compared different airline prices and routing options. I have to go to a meeting in San Diego next week, and I spent an hour on that alone last night, checking out flights and different hotels in the area.

Now, think about how much time in the last year you really sat down and looked at or organized your finances. If you're like most people, you probably spent more time planning that one vacation. Vacations are very important to both your mental and physical health (people who take regular vacations live longer than those who don't), but if your financial health really needs your attention, I believe that that's more important. After all, you have to pay for that vacation with something (and I don't just mean a credit card).

Do you go into debt to give generous gifts to others? Have you taken the time to find a good accountant or advisor for your financial life, or have you handed over your financial life to a "financial planner" who seems to be more interested in selling you financial products than in truly planning your financial success? Do you charge things to your credit cards, day after day, because "someday" you'll figure out how to pay them all off?

When we live like this—and so many of us do—deep down we know that we're doing ourselves a major disservice. That awareness clutters the back of our minds, creating an unease that we can't shake, which grows over time. Later, we complain that we can't seem to get ahead financially. Taking time to understand, organize, and plan your finances is an important aspect of loving yourself.

Thankfully, the fundamentals of a successful and less-stressful financial life are really quite simple:

❧ *Get real about the numbers*

Just like any other part of your life that you might be having difficulty with, becoming aware of the reality of your situation is the first and most powerful step.

One of the most illuminating steps can be simply keeping track of all your expenses, big and small, for one month. Often when we plan our budgets, we take into account our major regular expenses, such as your rent or mortgage payment, car payments, and the electric or phone bills. You may not realize that you spend $100 a month on your morning coffee or $200 a month on after-work drinks with your coworkers. When you write down everything you spend, and see the grand total on paper, you might suddenly understand why you always seem to have too much month left at the end of your money.

❧ *Organize and automate*

If you're constantly late paying certain bills, arrange to have the amount automatically debited from your checking account. For bills that you have to pay yourself, make a highlighted note in your agenda several days before it's due, or set up an alarm on your cell phone or electronic organizer. Or, better yet, have one day every month when you pay all your bills at once.

If you're always late depositing your paychecks into your bank account (despite needing the money), ask if your employer can set up a direct deposit. If you really want to start saving, but can't seem to get in the habit, set up an automatic monthly withdrawal from your checking account into a savings account or retirement plan.

❧ *Treat your money and other people's money with respect*

In my own financial journey, one of the most important things I learned is that money and debt are much more than mere dollar signs in our lives. The way you handle money and the way you handle your financial relationships are often symbolic of how you live the rest of your life.

Financial interactions involving family and friends are the ones that we need to treat most carefully. Despite this, they're often the financial relationships that we treat the most casually or disrespectfully.

Have you ever lent money to someone close to you who promised to pay you back but never did? When I was thirteen, a friend from school asked me to lend her money so that she could buy a concert ticket. I actually had to borrow the money from my father, in order to buy our two tickets. She never did pay me back, but I still remember her showing up at school wearing an expensive pair of new shoes the following week!

If you've borrowed money from someone close to you and you can't pay it all back right now, set up an installment plan, even if you can only give them a small amount each week. The same goes for any other creditors you have—ask about creating a manageable payment plan, and ask them if they'll give you a break on interest rates. You'd be amazed at what the people and companies you owe money to may be willing to agree to. When you show people that you're willing to honor your commitments to them, it can do wonders for the health of both your finances and the relationship.

❧ *Give thanks by giving to those in need*

This one might take some extra courage and faith, but if you can, follow the spiritual principle of giving 10 percent of what you earn to people or causes who need it more than you do. I've heard countless of stories of people who started doing this kind of "tithing" during times of personal financial crisis, who were later amazed by the amount of emotional, spiritual, and financial abundance that began to pour into their lives.

Giving to those who are in need, while simultaneously tending your own financial garden, is wonderful for both your mental and physical health. Respecting, taking care of, and sharing the money and abundance that come into your life is an essential part of creating a healthy relationship with yourself and your whole life.

REACH OUT FOR STRENGTH AND HELP ALONG THE WAY

In this chapter we've talked about many elements that make up self-love: pursuing real solutions instead of just filling ourselves with temporary "quick fixes," choosing healthy rewards, making time to take care of ourselves, reducing clutter, and addressing our finances proactively to improve our lives.

I've worked hard on all these areas of my life, though I still have work to do in each. These deliberate acts of healthy self-love have made such a huge difference to my quality of life, and to the kind of life and people that I experience and seem to attract.

But even with all this "wisdom," I would be lying if I didn't admit that I've had a lot of help along the way. I've attended support groups, have had many wonderful friends, mentors, and teachers, and have said a lot of prayers along the way, asking for help.

As I mentioned earlier, for almost any area of life that you are struggling with there are books, groups, websites, counselors, and specialty coaches that help people just like you heal and move forward with life. Some resources you can even get for free, such as library books, online articles, and support groups that are funded by donations.

When you take even the smallest baby steps towards loving yourself and putting various areas of your life in loving, respectful order, wonderful changes will begin to occur. I've discovered that whenever I make the choice to be truly kind to myself, even if, or especially if, it involves some kind of sacrifice or risk, I've noticed again and again that life pours down all kinds of gifts and surprises on me afterwards.

Also, the more I focus on living a life in which I treat myself and others with love, truth, and integrity, the better I feel about both myself and my life, and the better life seems to go.

Be very kind to yourself. Be patient with yourself. Believe in yourself and believe in the change that you can and will create in your life, one step and one day at a time. It all begins with you. Be good to yourself and you'll have more good to share with others. The rest will all fall into place.

4

MASTER THE ART OF RECEIVING

WHEN SOMETHING GOOD knocks at your door, do you open up wide and let it in? Many of us say and believe that we want more love, affection, and abundance in our lives, but when they show up we suddenly get nervous, or uncomfortable, or feel guilty, and block it or push it away.

One of my coaching clients is a charismatic, highly accomplished person, loved by everyone who knows her. Unfortunately, she has almost no time for herself and over-commits herself so much that you rarely ever see her sit down because she's already late for her next commitment.

She's the only client in the history of my practice who has managed to drive, cook, and eat, all during a single coaching session. Normally I insist that clients block off the time and find a quiet, private place to talk where they won't be interrupted. She had promised me that she'd clear her schedule for our hour together, but as usual, life and its demands crowded in.

Like many others that I've worked with, she doesn't have boundaries when it comes to letting other people's needs, plans, and demands invade her life and peace of mind. She gives freely of her money, time, and expertise, but it's a one-way street. She won't stop giving, helping, and doing long enough to let anything else in. Giving is wonderful for your physical and emotional health, but if you don't give yourself a chance to stop and recharge, it turns into a formula for disaster.

When her life became so chaotic and exhausting that she came to me for help, we had to work hard on three main areas: 1) learning to say no, 2) asking others for help, and 3) allowing that help into her life without feeling guilty or like a failure.

Most cultures place a high value on people who give generously. I agree with that opinion, but some people who don't see or believe in their own unconditional worth take the practice too far. They give endlessly, without healthy boundaries, to both appear and feel good, and they run themselves into the ground in the process.

Giving *is* a wonderful and essential part of a meaningful, healthy life. But here's the twist: so is *receiving*.

My friend Jessica, an extremely busy small business owner, loves her employees and they love her. Everyone who works for her knows that they can approach her any time for great advice about any challenge in their lives, be it professional or personal. Jessica gives joyfully and very generously—but she's almost completely unable to receive.

She works extremely hard, and those who receive from her often want to give something back. She often jokes about needing to spend an entire week in a spa, so her employees constantly give her spa certificates as gifts. Wouldn't you like to have her "problem"? She actually has accumulated enough certificates to go to a different spa, every day of the week, for an entire week without paying for it!

But she doesn't use the certificates. Some of them have even expired (a tragedy so great, I can't even fathom it). She could find the time if she wanted to, and constantly talks about how much she needs to stop, relax, and take better care of herself, but she just can't take the next step. She has all the time in the world for everyone else, but as much as she talks about needing the spa, it seems impossible for her to pick up the phone, make the *free* appointment, and go.

So many people who find it easy to give to others find it difficult to accept help and gifts from the very same people, or anyone else. And when it comes to nurturing themselves and taking care of themselves, forget it!

Another behavior I've observed is that people seem to automatically spend money on things that they see other people buying, such as new wide-screen TVs and the latest brand-name clothes and accessories. Meanwhile, they won't spend money on items and activities that might truly benefit their lives in a lasting, healthy way. A naturopathic doctor I know once pointed out that most people spend more money on their cars than on their own health. She's right! Isn't that nuts?

And yes, by the way, going to the spa *does* qualify as a way of taking care of your health. Massages have been shown to stimulate the immune system, decrease stress, improve circulation, decrease pain, and even significantly decrease the symptoms of PMS. So buy yourself a gift certificate, write your name on it, and *don't* let it expire.

SMILE AND SAY "THANK YOU"

How do you feel when you find something that would make an absolutely perfect gift for a good friend? If it's a particularly amazing gift, I usually can't wait until the special occasion to give it to them, so I come up with some reason why I "have to" give it to them right away.

Now let's flip this around: What if *you* were the person receiving the gift in the above example? Would you say something like this: "You shouldn't have! I can't accept this! What did you go and do that for?"

If you're a mother from a certain generation (I know this because I now have two), you might even scold the giver, saying that the gift is too expensive or fancy for you, that you know you won't use it, and that they should take it back for a refund and find a better use for their hard-earned money. (Sigh.)

And what about the epidemic of check-grabbing witnessed in restaurants? The bill arrives, and the first person to see it says: "Let me get the bill." On cue, the others erupt into protest: "No, let me get it!" or "At the very least, we have to split it!"

These statements are usually followed by a tug-of-war across the table, with each person, or several people, trying to extract the bill folder from the vise-like grip of the other. I know this because I've done it, and have been both the bill-payer and the bill-grabber. The worst part is that if I "lose" the battle in the end, and the other person ends up paying, I've often been so distracted by the check drama that I forget, in the end, to say thank you.

Here's the thing: When someone gives you something, *they* benefit—emotionally, spiritually, and physically. And guess what? No one can experience the benefits of giving unless there's some-one who's willing to receive what they want to give.

If someone wants to pick up the check at a restaurant, let them—with a smile, gratitude and grace. If someone gives you a gift, receive it and thank them sincerely. Focus on the gift, and tell them how much and why you appreciate it, rather than focusing on why they "shouldn't have."

If someone offers to help you, let them. If you need help, ask for it. If someone gives you a compliment, accept it and let the truth of it light you up inside. By happily receiving, you add light to the giver's life, too.

DO UNTO OTHERS, BUT DON'T FORGET YOURSELF!

We all know the Golden Rule: "Do unto others as you would have done unto you." I have a similar saying that I made up to help my pathologically helpful coaching clients: "Do unto yourself as you would do unto others."

I know a woman who is famous for her elaborate dinner parties. She spends hours, even days, planning, shopping for, and creating meals that people rave about for weeks. She loves food, but when she's at home alone, she frequently finds it "too much of a bother" to even make herself a sandwich. Her refrigerator is usually empty, and some nights, she won't even have dinner. After some time spent working with a therapist, she finally understood that the contradiction between her treatment of others and her care for herself dramatically reflected her own lack of self-love and self-worth.

Treat yourself the same way that you would treat anyone you care deeply about. Give yourself time, patience, love, kindness, and thoughtful, loving gifts and treats. Instead of feeling guilty, receive those acts of self-love with a smile and a deep feeling of gratitude.

If you let more love, help, and prosperity in, your own cup will spill over with love and abundance. Then you'll have a constantly renewable supply of love and abundance to bless the lives of the others with. And remember: Graciously receiving the help, love, and gifts that others wish to give to you is actually a powerfully effective way of directly blessing the people you care about.

3

HONOR YOUR BODY

5

LEARN YOUR BODY'S LANGUAGE

I WAS IN MEXICO when I got the email. It came from Maria's manager, telling me that my friend had collapsed after her show the night before. There were still several dates left on the tour, but since the collapse had happened while they were performing in a city only ten hours south of Toronto, Maria's hometown, the tour bus was at that very moment driving her towards the border to get her to a Canadian hospital.

I'd gotten an email from Maria just a few days prior. A dancer with a huge stage production, she'd just finished a grueling tour of Europe, and was doing a few dates across the United States before finally coming home.

"I think I have a bladder infection," she wrote. "I've had the symptoms for about a week, and they're not getting better. I've been keeping the pain under control by drinking cranberry juice all day long. What should I do? I'll be home in another couple of weeks—can I wait until then to see a doctor?"

I wrote Maria back immediately, telling her to see a doctor right away. She decided to wait until the next day. By the time she was on that bus, rocketing towards the border, she had a high fever and was delirious. The pain in her back, which she'd had for days, had gotten so bad that she could barely move. If she'd emailed me about her back pain (which I wish she had), I would have told her that her kidney was infected and that she needed immediate treatment.

The doctors in the emergency room in Canada took one look at Maria and hospitalized her. When I spoke to her a few hours later, she was groggy from morphine and still in so much pain that she could hardly speak. They had diagnosed her with a severe abscess of her kidney, and were going to have to operate to drain it.

If Maria had waited a few days more to get help, she could have died.

Maria, like so many of us, has way too many things to do during any given day in her life. She's constantly running from meeting to rehearsal to show to meeting, and hasn't taken a real vacation in years. The Marias of the world—and there are many these days—don't have time to eat properly, much less find the time for the "inconvenience" of seeing a doctor.

SENDING OUT AN S.O.S.

We come equipped with a brilliant messaging system, and almost anyone can easily master the basics. Unfortunately, after working with thousands of patients, from celebrities to homeless people, I can confidently say that most people, like Maria, don't pay much attention to this system. Or, if they do notice the blinking red light, they ignore it or pretend they don't see it and keep right on going.

It's really quite a fair, user-friendly system. If you're up to something that could ultimately threaten your health, your body will first whisper to you, giving you some gentle hints. You might feel a little more tired or irritable. Your allergies might start to act up. You might develop a mild rash or catch the sniffles for a day or two.

If you keep motoring on, your body will raise its voice to a higher decibel level. You might get hit with a cold that you can't seem to shake, get slowed down by a minor yet annoying injury, or feel plagued by increasing fatigue.

I see so many patients who are at this stage, usually at least a dozen a day when I'm working at the clinic. When I ask them whether they're taking proper care of themselves, or whether their lives are too busy, most of them just say: "Look, I really can't miss one more day of work. I appreciate your concern, but I need you to give me something to fix me, or at least to help get me through this. I've got way too much to do—I don't have time to be sick!"

"Sure," I say. "This antibiotic/decongestant/cough suppressant (whatever it is) will help you feel better. But that doesn't change the fact that you need to pay attention to your body and give it a chance to recover. Take some time to rest and look after yourself. If you don't, it'll take you longer to get over this, and you'll probably find yourself sick again soon. And next time, it'll probably be even worse."

They may or may not remember my words when they hit the next stage. Or, rather, when the next stage hits them. This time it might be an all-out flu or pneumonia that keeps them in bed for a week. Or it could be something much more serious, like what happened to Maria.

I am not saying that it's always your fault if you get sick. Life and health don't always work that way and there are always going to be mysteries that we can't explain. People with very healthy, well-balanced lives can suddenly get diagnosed with some terrible illness, and no one can figure out why.

Still, in most situations when you get sick, there probably is *something* that you could have done that might have prevented your body from getting into that situation. If not, you might at least have been able to decrease the severity of your eventual symptoms. If you're in tune with your body, and deeply respect its early warning system and the symptoms and signs that go with that, then you are much more likely to catch, diagnose, and even fix the problem in its earliest and more easily treatable stages.

If you do get sick, it's not too late. You can still use the experience to guide you into the essential changes you may need to make with respect to the way you treat your body and your life. As a result, you can profoundly change both your experience of that illness and, possibly, its outcome.

No matter what pessimists may tell you, there is always something positive that you can learn from your body and any illness it experiences. Once you figure out what that lesson is, you can immediately begin applying it in a positive way to improve your life and, ideally, the lives of others as well.

ACCIDENTAL WISDOM

In my first year of medical school, we were all revved-up and bright-eyed, eager to become the next great masters of our profession. Every second counted, and the scent of competition filled the air.

One morning, a group of us bustled into our assigned room. This was the first of our small-group clinical teaching sessions with a real live doctor from the community. We snuck side-glances at him, and he looked like the real thing: glasses, gray hair, and a white lab coat.

But then he opened his mouth. He started by asking us if any of us had ever had an accident. One of my classmates was a former motorcycle racer, and he volunteered the story of how an unexpected fall during a race had injured his back and destroyed his career.

"Why do you think that happened?" asked our professor. We all looked at each other.

"What do you mean, why?" the student asked, puzzled. "It was an accident, it just happened and that was it."

The professor smiled. "Let me explain the question a little bit better. What I'm asking you is why did that accident happen at that point in your life? What was the reason for it? *Why* did it happen?"

The student was getting seriously annoyed. "I told you, it was an accident. Are you trying to say I ended my career on purpose? That's ridiculous!" We were all laughing by then—at the professor.

Our teacher went on to explain. He told us that the reason he had asked *why* the injury had happened was because he had learned, through decades of practicing medicine, that there was usually some kind of greater meaning, or message, in almost any illness, and even in seemingly accidental injuries.

Now we were really worried. We wanted to learn about "real" medicine, not strange personal philosophies. We needed practical information that we could actually use in our professional lives. At the very least, we wanted to learn something we could use to pass our exams.

I have no idea what the other students think now, almost fifteen years after that class. Today, I appreciate that he may have been one of the wisest teachers in that entire faculty. I've practiced medicine for almost ten years now, and I've observed many times what that professor was talking about. He wasn't kidding about those accidents.

Last year, I filled in for another doctor in a medical clinic downtown. A couple of hours into the day, I opened the examining room door to find a worried-looking woman sitting in a wheelchair. I assumed she was disabled, until she told me her story.

"I'm here on business from San Francisco and I fell while I was getting off the ferry," she told me. "Both of my ankles are killing me, and I can't walk. I'm a speaker and I have to give a bunch of seminars while I'm here, so I need to get better, fast. Can you help me?"

Anyone would have compassion for a person who can't walk because they've injured both of their ankles, but the fact that she, like me, was a professional speaker helped me immediately relate to the stress of her situation. People think that being a speaker just involves standing in front of an audience and being paid really well to talk for an hour. They don't know about the extensive and exhausting travel, preparations, and details involved.

When I asked her what kind of speaking she did, I discovered that the woman in front of me was publicity guru Jill Lublin, the best-selling author of the book *Guerrilla Publicity*.

"Is your life normally really busy?" I asked her.

She rolled her eyes and laughed. "Honey, you have no idea. That's why this is so terrible—this can't happen to me now. I have too much to do, too many people I'm going to disappoint. I don't have time for this! I don't have time to go to a hospital. I'm sure I'm fine, please just tell me I'll be fine, and if you could also give me something for the pain, that would be fabulous."

I pulled my chair up next to her wheelchair.

"Do you think that maybe this happened to you because you need to slow down?"

She stared at me for a moment, and then laughed again. "You sound just like Gail, that's what she told me, too."

Gail turned out to be a friend of Jill's who lives in Vancouver and also happened to be organizing one of the events that Jill was supposed to speak at. Gail had picked Jill up at the ferry terminal shortly after the accident and taken her to a downtown hotel (which was just a couple of blocks from the clinic). Apparently, during the entire ride to the hotel, Gail lectured Jill about the fact that this entire accident was nothing more than a sign that she needed to slow down.

When it first happened to her, Jill's injury felt more like an unwelcome, agonizingly painful crisis than a cosmic intervention for her own good. Both of her ankles did turn out to have hairline fractures, and she was immobilized in a wheelchair for several weeks.

During that time, she couldn't do most of the things that she normally took for granted. Forced to slow down, she suddenly had plenty of time to reflect on the pace and direction of her life, and the reason why this had happened. Despite all her pain and frustration and lost income, she began to see the great blessing in it all. Today she actually incorporates her "accidental" experience into her speaking presentations; in fact, I personally heard her talk about it at a conference of the National Speakers Association (NSA).

"One day, on a speaking trip to Vancouver, I literally got stopped in my tracks," she begins, and then shares her story of what happened. She's even planning to write an entire book about her experience.

I also remember hearing the surprising success story of a well-known Canadian singer, Chantal Kreviazuk. A classically trained piano prodigy, she was seriously injured in a scooter accident in Italy in 1984. She was immobilized for several months afterwards, and during that time spontaneously began composing and singing pop songs. Though she had never performed live as a vocalist, she approached Sony records with her work, and shortly after signed one of the biggest deals in Canadian music history. Though she was probably very upset when her scooter crashed and wrecked her trip to Italy, I imagine that she, just like Jill, now looks back at it as one of the best things that ever happened to her.

HEAL YOUR LIFE, HEAL YOUR BODY

Brenda suffered in an abusive, oppressive marriage for most of her adult life. During that time, she developed frequent sore throats. They took swabs, cultures, and blood tests, and at one point she even saw a specialist. No one could tell her why this kept happening, nor could anyone fix it.

One day, Brenda finally found the courage to leave her cruel, controlling husband. Shortly after, she awoke one morning and noticed that her painful throat symptoms had disappeared. When she thought about it, she realized that her throat hadn't hurt for weeks. Here's how she explained this "miracle" to me:

"For years, I wasn't allowed to voice my opinions or speak up for myself," she told me. "As soon as I got my life and my 'voice' back, the sore throats went away, forever."

It could be that the constant stress of an abusive marriage had compromised Brenda's immune system, resulting in persistent throat inflammation or a mysteriously undetectable infection. Another possibility would be that the constant tension in her life caused excess production of stomach acid, which washed up into her throat as she slept at night, burning and irritating her delicate throat tissues. Other mind-body experts might say that the area of the throat is symbolic of our ability to express ourselves: when your voice is suppressed, that area becomes sick.

No matter which theory may be right, Brenda's healing still demonstrates that her persistent sore throat was a symptom of what was wrong with her life. All the throat lozenges in the world could never have been as effective as removing, or transforming, that situation in her life that literally had her by the throat.

The other day, after I finished a speaking presentation, a woman named Margaret came up to me and told me her story. She used to work eighty-hour weeks, flitting from one airline lounge to another as a high-flying corporate executive.

"I'd have a breakfast meeting in London and a dinner meeting in New York. It was crazy, but I loved the rush of it all, and the power of making a big deal," she told me.

As the demands and the deals got tougher, Margaret continued to push her body beyond its reasonable limits. She became more and more exhausted, which she at first assumed was just cumulative jet lag. Finally, her whole body started to hurt, to the point that she couldn't get out of bed anymore. Her doctor's diagnosis: fibromyalgia, a debilitating and poorly understood chronic pain disorder.

Unable to continue in her intense career, Margaret had to leave her job. Since her doctors couldn't do much for her, other than prescribing painkillers, she started searching for causes of her new, baffling illness. When she identified both electrical and chemical contaminants in her home, she decided to sell it and create a new non-toxic, healthy home environment to see if it would help her illness. Over time, her fibromyalgia symptoms did disappear.

She began a new part-time career helping people design toxin-free homes and continued to enjoy excellent health and energy. One afternoon, she got a call from a colleague from her previous job in the corporate world. He offered her a lucrative short-term contract.

"I thought I might as well try it," she told me. "I'd enjoyed the work when I was doing it and assumed that I'd just worked too hard the first time around. By then, I also thought that the majority of my illness had been due to the contaminants in my home."

She accepted the contract, and went back to work. To her surprise, the fatigue and body aches of fibromyalgia returned, in just a matter of weeks.

This time, Margaret quickly diagnosed the problem: "My body told me, in no uncertain terms, that I simply wasn't supposed to be in that world anymore, no matter how much I'd once liked it."

She got the message, and has put corporate life behind her for good. Instead, she's enjoying happiness, good health, and doing what she was really meant to do.

YOU ALREADY HAVE THE ANSWER

The next time something happens in your body, whether it's something minor or a more serious event (including an accident), ask yourself what it might really be about. We doctors know a lot, but when it comes to what needs changing in your own life, you're the expert. We can tell you what's going wrong physically with your cells and tissues and can offer a variety of practical medical solutions to treat the problem, but you have access to the most important information: your own natural wisdom and insight.

I get frustrated when I see people going to psychics or healers, trying to discover "the true meaning" behind this illness or that life event. It bothers me because, as I've already mentioned, you are by far the most likely person to be able to figure out the true purpose behind what is happening to you.

Other people's opinions or predictions can confuse you and lead you astray, or make you think that you're not capable of reaching your own conclusions. I speak from experience because I, too, used to be one of those people who thought that I needed to go to other people to get explanations for what was happening in my life and health.

Aside from wasting your money, another danger of going to others for answers is that we humans are very suggestible. A thirty-something friend of mine was once told by a healer (who had never examined her physically) that she had a very thin, distended bowel wall that she would probably die from in the next few years. My friend didn't want to worry her family, so she didn't tell anyone what she had been told. For a week, she lay awake at night, unable to sleep. She also stopped eating solid foods because she didn't want to irritate her vulnerable bowels. Luckily, we ran into each other at mutual friend's house and she pulled me aside to tell me the horrible news.

When I told her that I thought the "diagnosis" was ridiculous, she burst into tears and hugged me. Because she'd been so worried, I encouraged her to talk to her own physician about her concerns. Of course, she's turned out to be just fine.

If your body develops a new symptom or illness, first go see your doctor for assessment, diagnosis, and advice. However, in addition to that, I'd like you to ask yourself: What is this *really* about?

What might your body be trying to tell you? Is there something new (or old) going on in your life that may have triggered this? Has this happened to you before, and can you see a pattern? Is there something in your life that you need to approach differently, or perhaps get rid of? Is this some kind of a wake-up call? What might happen if you ignore it and just keep going?

Spend some quiet time alone and reflect on what's going on. You might say a prayer, and ask for guidance. Or you might take some time to write in your journal about what's going on in your body and your life and see what thoughts and insights appear as you write.

It's totally natural to experience grief, anger, or self-pity when things go wrong with your health. Yet, if you choose to look for the lesson, or the message, or the gift, in whatever happens to or in your body, it'll change your experience of illness forever. I guarantee that you'll discover that most if not all of the "tragedies" that arrive in your life eventually lead to some kind of happy or meaningful ending.

Your body is your best friend. Listen to it, care for it, honor it, and take its messages seriously. After all, achieving your dreams won't mean much if you don't have the energy and health to properly enjoy them.

6

LOOK GOOD, FEEL FABULOUS: THE ANTI-AGING, HEALING POWER OF FOODS

*H*OW DO YOU feel about the foods that you usually eat? Could you be making better choices? Would you like to learn how to choose foods that will help you achieve your ideal weight, have more energy, or slow down the aging progress? I'm pretty sure I can guess your answer!

I've been studying nutrition for over twenty years—I have a university degree in Dietetics, and I wrote a monthly nutrition column for Canada's doctors and health care professionals for eight years. People refer to me as a "health and dietary expert," and the media often ask me for quotes or information on the subject of nutrition.

Even though I've got these credentials and all this knowledge, I still face many of the same dietary challenges that you do. Some days (many days) I *still* have a hard time getting in the "recommended daily amounts" of fruits, vegetables, and high-quality protein. I also have to remind myself regularly to eat something healthy, rather than the handful of cookies that I'd prefer (sometimes I do let myself have the cookies). So I can only imagine how challenging it might be for you to eat well.

By sharing with you the secrets that help me, every day, to conquer my natural food tendencies (a powerful preference for cookies and chocolate cake), I'm hoping that I'll be able to make a significant difference in the way you eat, the way you look, the rate at which you age, *and* the quality of life and health that you experience.

IF THE FACTS DON'T MOTIVATE YOU, MAYBE VANITY WILL?

I'm pretty sure that if I stopped almost anyone on the street and asked them to list a few examples of healthy foods, they'd be able to. I find it hard to believe that anyone honestly thinks that a giant cheeseburger and fries is a healthy, balanced food choice. So why do we, as a culture, eat so much junk, and so little of the healthy stuff?

You probably already know that regular consumption of unhealthy foods can increase your risk of heart disease, diabetes, high cholesterol, and even cancer. I'm not going to dwell on that here because you've heard all that before, and if you're like most people, that knowledge alone hasn't done much to change your eating habits. (By the way, even if you do think that you eat well already, I think you'll find out some interesting things from this chapter that will make it worth sticking around!)

Most of my life, I've had a fairly healthy diet, give or take a few horrific childhood cereals (if your favorite cereal is colored pink, purple, red, or any combination of the three, you may want to choose another brand). Still, over the years I've regularly eaten plenty of things that I knew weren't good for me, and had a hard time kicking some unhealthy habits.

What finally "cured" me of those habits was observing the huge effect that certain foods have on how I both look and feel. I promise you, you'll be amazed at the effect that simple changes in your diet can have on your face, and the rate that you age in the mirror. (Have I got your attention now?)

I must warn you that there's a major side effect of this way of eating: The food choices that make you more beautiful and give you more energy also happen to be the foods that protect your body from illness and biological aging. So, are you with me?

THE CLEAR SKIN DIARIES

I've been plagued by acne since I was a teenager. But even if you've been blessed with clear skin your entire life, I assure you that my story will still be relevant to you.

When I was in my second year of medical school, my skin suddenly took a dramatic turn for the worse, presumably due to stress. When topical treatments failed, my dermatologist put me on Accutane, an extremely powerful medication that wiped out my acne completely. It was like a miracle.

A few years later, when I started working in clinics, my face started to break out again. Again, I assumed it was caused by stress. However, a weird thing happened when I went on a trip to Italy. You'd think that that vacation would have relieved my stress, but I came back looking like a pizza. My skin looked so bad that one day at work, one of the other doctors actually asked me: "What happened to your face?" (By the way, please don't ever say that to anyone in a similar situation. It's not very nice.)

I went to another dermatologist, went back on Accutane, and my skin cleared up again—until I moved to Mexico. That was a pretty big life change, so I again assumed that stress was my fundamental problem. As I settled into my new Mexican life, my stress level improved but my skin got worse. During one of my trips back home, I saw yet another dermatologist. Dr. James Dantow turned out to be way ahead of his time and forever changed the way I understood the relationship between the food I eat and the health of my skin.

In medical school, they taught us that diet has absolutely no relationship to acne. That old-school view is now changing, thanks to researchers around the world. In addition to well-designed studies that have found a relationship between acne and certain foods, they've also documented cultures where acne simply doesn't exist. One of the primary differences between these cultures and the rest of the world is their diet.

Dr. Dantow listened to my acne history and asked me if I'd changed my way of eating in Mexico. I was surprised to realize that I had. Back home in Canada, I'd half-heartedly followed a wheat-free, dairy-free diet for several years, on the advice of a naturopath.

When I got to Mexico, they didn't have my usual wheat and dairy substitutes, and I celebrated my great escape by indulging in all kinds of treats that I hadn't eaten for years: ice cream, flour tortillas, pancakes, chocolate bars, toast, jam, sugary yogurt drinks, the list goes on. I'd done the same on my trip to Italy, abandoning my usual diet for large quantities of gelato, pasta, and baskets of crusty white bread.

"I don't think stress is your main problem, though it certainly makes things worse," said Dr. Dantow. He gave me a list of potential problem foods for acne patients and handed me a note from his prescription pad.

"Read this book," he told me.

I went straight to the library and checked out dermatologist Nicholas Perricone's book: *The Perricone Prescription.*

More on that in a moment, but before I continue I'd like to let you know that from this point onwards I won't say much more about acne, other than that Dr. Dantow and Dr. Perricone finally gave me back control of my skin. If you, like me, are an adult who can't believe that you *still* can't leave the house without a cover-up stick, I also recommend the book *The Clear Skin Diet,* by naturopath Alan Logan and dermatologist Valori Treloar. You can also find a summary article about the most powerful aspects of this diet in the articles section of my website, www.susanbiali.com.

THE INFLAMMATION CONNECTION

In his best-selling *Prescription,* Dr. Perricone, who taught at Yale, describes young women with sagging, prematurely aging faces. According to Perricone, "the signs of aging—including wrinkling, crepey skin, sagging jawline and jowls, drooping eyelids, under-eye bags, and puffiness—are all the results of inflammation."

Years prior, Perricone studied various skin and body cell types under a microscope and noticed that all the older, unhealthy cells shared a common feature: they were packed with smaller inflammatory cells. Perricone reached the conclusion that many chronic disease researchers were also beginning to make: inflammation is associated with, and may be the cause of, most of our major diseases. As a dermatologist, Perricone took this observation a step further. He hypothesized that this inflammation was simultaneously accelerating the aging of our skin.

It turns out that certain foods cause inflammation, disease, and aging in our body cells and in our skin, while other foods reduce inflammation and may even reverse some of the damage. Perricone's "Wrinkle-Free Diet" is essentially what other experts are now calling an "Anti-Inflammatory Diet." I'm telling you about Perricone's version because most people (including me) tend to be more motivated by the idea of preventing wrinkles and aging than about

consciously turning down the level of inflammation in their bodies—even though the two are pretty much one and the same.

I have to comment here that I generally avoid using the word
"diet" because so many people associate that four-letter-word with
short-term sacrifice, suffering, and eventual failure. This isn't a diet
in the typical sense of the word; rather, it's simply a life-long way
of eating that has remarkable benefits for your looks and your
health.

As I mentioned earlier, eating this way has some wonderful side
effects. According to Perricone: "You will experience increased
vitality, sharpened cognitive and problem-solving skills, and
improved memory." Think you can handle that?

Since Perricone's detailed prescription fills several hundred
pages, I've condensed this anti-inflammatory diet into five basic
elements (I'll elaborate more in a moment):

- Regularly feed your body high-quality proteins (e.g., fish,
  egg whites, skinless chicken breast)
- Eat plenty of "good" fats (e.g., olive oil and the omega-3
  fats found in salmon)
- Avoid "bad" fats (e.g., hydrogenated trans fats found in
  bakery goods, margarines, and fried foods; saturated fats
  found in red meat)
- Eat less high-glycemic refined carbohydrates (e.g., white
  flour, sugar, rice, pasta, potatoes)
- Eat more low-glycemic high-fiber carbohydrates (e.g.,
  oatmeal, whole grains, apples, berries)

Perricone also recommends taking a number of supplements. In
my opinion, since we don't really understand the long-term consequences and benefits of taking these different nutrient and food
extracts, I prefer sticking to good old healthy food.

THE ALL-IMPORTANT GLYCEMIC INDEX

Foods that get quickly converted to sugar in your body are said to have a high glycemic index (GI). White flour, sugary foods, white rice, potatoes, sweet drinks and juices, and even sweet fruits like bananas and mangos fall into this category. The high levels of blood sugar that result when you eat these foods cause inflammation in your cells and can lead to acne breakouts, premature aging, and damage to your body's organs.

One thing Perricone pointed out in his book has stuck with me forever. High-carbohydrate foods translate directly into high levels of sugar in your body. That sugar enters your skin cells and starts cross-linking your collagen. Drum roll: This heralds the first phase of wrinkle generation. On top of that, the high sugar levels suck water into your cells, causing your face to puff up, most noticeably around your eyes.

The next time you have a big plate of pasta for dinner, look closely at your face the next morning. Do you see what I'm talking about?

Imagine the long-term effect on your skin, spending all night, every night, puffed up and stretched out like that. You might not notice it now, but you will if you start replacing high GI foods with low GI substitutes (see the Appendix for some "Prescription for Healthy Eating" Menus and Tips, including a description of what I eat in a typical day. You'll also find more extensive, continually updated information and articles on my website, www.susanbiali.com). You'll wish you knew about all this years ago! It's never too late, though, and according to Perricone, some of these changes, such as a jowly sagging face, can improve dramatically if you simply start eating right.

Now think of how tired you look the morning after drinking too much wine or way too many martinis. In small amounts, wine is good for your body, but any more than a glass or two and you'll wake up a little older, biologically speaking, than when you went to bed. How fun is that?

Now, let's talk in more detail about the magical foods that may actually slow down time, and in some cases, according to Perricone, may even turn it back.

Whenever you can, eat high-fiber foods. Most vegetables, other than potatoes and sweet potatoes, have a low glycemic index and are powerfully anti-inflammatory in their own right, thanks to high levels of antioxidants and other nutrients. Eat as much as you want of low GI fruits, including apples, berries, cherries, plums, peaches, oranges, and grapefruits. Avoid eating handfuls of dried fruits; according to Perricone, these contain very high concentrations of fructose, which loves to attach itself to your collagen.

Online, you'll find lists of high and low glycemic index foods that can help you make better food choices (as mentioned, there's also a list of these on my website). But before I say any more, I'd like to make sure that you know that there's no need to follow this to the extreme. I tried Perricone's ultra-anti-inflammatory "Three-Day Nutritional Face-Lift," for more than three days. That week, when I told my clinic manager that I didn't want to go to the office Christmas party because I constantly felt like crying, she, a professional fitness competitor, asked me what I'd been eating.

When I told her, she laughed. "I knew it! You're eating the same diet that I do when I prepare for a competition. My husband actually moves out of the house every time I do it. You need to eat some more carbs, girl!"

She was right. Ever since then, I haven't given up favorites such as white rice, potatoes, and brown rice pasta. I just make sure that when I eat these higher GI foods, I eat smaller portions than I used to, and eat enough good quality protein, such as chicken or salmon, in the same meal. The protein slows down the rate at which the carbs get turned into sugar in my body, and adds to the anti-aging effect of my meal.

According to Perricone, many women who are constantly dieting don't get enough protein to maintain youthful-looking skin. We need to eat enough protein to help our cells repair themselves throughout the day. Many people, in the name of dieting, cut out (good) fat, skimp on protein sources, and just eat carbohydrates and vegetables all day. Don't be one of them!

Now, on to the most powerful anti-inflammatory food of all: fish. We've all heard about salmon and its wonderful omega-3 fatty acids. Did you know that in addition to protecting your heart, your mood, and your mind, salmon and other fish rich in omega-3 also prevent inflammation and aging? From a weight-loss point of view, fish is a fantastic food choice because it's nutrient dense. Every forkful of fish that you eat comes loaded with high-quality protein, healthy fats, antioxidants, and other vitamins and minerals. I love salmon, and eat it whenever I can.

Cook or flavor your foods with another dietary fountain of youth and health: extra virgin olive oil. This miraculous golden liquid can probably take much of the credit for the health benefits of the famous Mediterranean diet.

I only cook with olive oil, and use it as the basis for all my salad dressings. Dip your multi-grain breads into olive oil and balsamic vinegar instead of slathering them with butter or margarine. (Bonus nutrition tip: some studies have shown vinegar to be an appetite suppressant, so if you start a meal with a salad with oil-and-vinegar dressing, you may naturally end up eating less of the main dish—and less dessert afterwards.)

Stay away from pro-inflammatory trans fats whenever you can. These hide in commercial baked goods, fried foods, and hydrogenated fats such as certain margarines. Read food labels carefully when shopping to decide which food items make it into your grocery cart.

If you're not convinced yet, consider this: I once came across a study that looked at the amount of skin wrinkling on its subjects, comparing dietary factors and total sun exposure. The researchers found that people who ate more olive oil, vegetables, and high-fiber (low GI) legumes such as beans and lentils, had significantly less wrinkled skin. They also found that people who ate less butter, margarine, milk products, and sugar all had better skin.

As I mentioned, I still occasionally indulge in a cookie or a piece of cake, but ever since I learned about this way of eating, I try to make anti-inflammatory food choices whenever I can. I remind myself to eat a fruit or vegetable at every meal (and as snacks), use lots of olive oil, have essentially cut out all white flour products, and eat fish as often as I can.

I hope that so far you've found all this information useful, and also motivating. When I discovered that these healthy and delicious foods not only protect me from illness, but also keep me looking young, I had a major cause for celebration!

ADDITIONAL SIDE EFFECTS
OF ANTI-INFLAMMATORY FOODS

Another unexpected yet marvelous side effect of eating the anti-inflammatory way: If you're overweight, it will help you lose weight, and it will also help you maintain your ideal weight. This works by a similar mechanism as other "low-carb" diets (though I'm not at all an advocate of extreme low-carb eating).

If you regularly eat balanced quantities of good protein and healthy fats in combination with healthy carbohydrates, you'll naturally feel fuller and it'll take longer for you to feel hungry again after eating.

You'll also avoid those blood sugar crashes that can leave you feeling tired and hungry after eating a high-carbohydrate meal or snack.

And, as I mentioned earlier, when you eat this way your mind and body also feel wonderfully alert and full of energy. I don't notice it so much day-to-day, but I sure notice it whenever I abandon my healthy way of eating and spend a day, or several days, indulging in yummy inflammatory foods. After you've eaten the anti-inflammatory way for a while, you'll notice it too. When you wake up in the morning, not only will you look and feel puffy, but you'll feel like someone slipped a drug into your drink the night before. No, thank you! The benefits are so great and the true sacrifices so few that you'll find that it just gets easier and easier to eat this way.

FOR SUCCESS, START SMALL & KEEP IT SIMPLE

In my perfect world, I would be able to teach and motivate everyone (including myself) to eat nothing but healthy, wonderful foods, and we would all look and feel fabulous, all the time. I'm hoping that you've learned lots of practical things about healthy eating and its benefits from this chapter, but I also realize that you might be feeling a bit overwhelmed, particularly if your kitchen cupboards don't normally contain many of the healthy foods that I've been talking about.

I've worked with enough coaching clients to know that people often think that if they can't do it right, they may as well not try at all. I want to emphasize that when it comes to healthy eating, small changes count for a lot. In fact, small changes are usually the very best way to start. If you try to change everything you eat overnight, it can come as a shock to your schedule, your cooking skills, your taste buds, and even your pocketbook. That's partly why so many diets fail, because people try to make extreme changes all at once.

If right now you normally eat two servings of fruits and vegetables a day, just adding one more serving (by adding berries to your cereal, or an apple as a snack, or a salad to your dinner) will be great news for your body. If you just add in one apple a day to your normal diet, that's 365 apples in a year. Just that simple step alone would significantly increase the amount of top-notch antioxidants provided to your body over the course of the year.

Here are some simple ways you can make big improvements to your health and nutrition, without having to make dramatic changes to your lifestyle:

❧ *Eat Breakfast*

Taking the time for a simple breakfast comes with all sorts of benefits: You'll be more alert and productive; you'll eat less total calories, fat, and cholesterol during the rest of the day; you'll be more likely to lose weight successfully; and if you've recently lost weight, you'll be more likely to keep it off. If you normally eat nothing for breakfast, just eat something. If you're already in the habit of having a coffee and a muffin, add some kind of protein source (like yogurt) and a fruit or glass of juice to make it a more complete meal.

❧ *Make Small Substitutions*

One of the best ways to change the way you eat is to sneak it in a bit at a time so that you barely notice it. For example, if your breakfast right now is a plain white toasted bagel with heaps of butter and jam, you can start with small changes. Try a multigrain bagel instead, decrease the amount of butter you use by half, and buy a healthier jam that's made from real fruit and/or has less added sugar. Add a glass of skim milk (a protein source), and you're off to a good start. You can make these kinds of changes to improve almost anything you eat: decrease portion sizes, add in healthier substitutes, or add something healthy (like a fruit or vegetable) to what you're already normally eating.

❧ *Eliminate or Decrease Sugary Drinks*

This is usually one of the first tips that I give people, as this small step can have such a big impact on your health. Ideally, I'd love to see you replace those sugary drinks or sodas with water—that's what I drink all day. If that's too hard right now, try simply decreasing the amount you drink, or switch to a diet version that doesn't have added sugar.

If you love (or are addicted to) caffeinated soda, try a green tea drink instead. If you've got to have something sweet, drink juice (ideally a no-sugar-added type) rather than soda, as juice at least has some vitamins and antioxidants in it. Even if you just manage to reduce the amount of soda that you drink by half, that's fantastic. As long as you make some small change, you're moving in the right direction!

❧ *Eat Regularly Throughout The Day*

There's a reason that a typical work day is set up to allow time for coffee breaks—employers know that if you eat regularly throughout the day, you'll be in a better mood and mental state, and perform better on the job. Also, if you take time to eat breakfast, a mid-morning snack, lunch, a mid-afternoon snack, dinner, and perhaps a light snack in the evening, chances are that you won't get ravenously hungry at any point in the day.

When you avoid getting ravenously hungry, you're less likely to binge-eat or grab unhealthy or sugary snacks for a quick fix. A good rule of thumb is to eat something (ideally a healthy something), every time you notice that you're starting to get hungry. Also, as I mentioned earlier, if you make the effort to eat solid meals that contain a balance of carbohydrates, protein, and fat, it'll take longer for you to get hungry again.

Come up with some ideas for healthy snacks and meals that you'd enjoy, and plan to have them handy so they're there when you need them. I almost always carry a granola bar in my purse!

WHETHER YOU'RE LOOKING for more of these kinds of simple tips or more sophisticated ways to rev up your nutritional health, you can find articles and blog posts about lots of different aspects of food and nutrition (including healthy weight loss) on my website, www.susanbiali.com.

4

RESCUE AND REVITALIZE YOUR RELATIONSHIPS

7

HAPPILY EVER AFTER

I'M NOT SURE when it was that I decided that the one essential ingredient that I needed to experience true happiness in this lifetime was the perfect man. In my search for "the one," I was rarely single for long. Unfortunately, the people whom I ended up dating and the difficult relationships that I experienced usually proved to be a very long way from the perfection that I was looking for.

People would ask, behind my back and occasionally right in front of me: "What is someone like *her* doing with someone like *him?*" These days, I'm more likely to be the one asking that question as I observe the choices of clients and other people around me.

I think that there were two main reasons for my behavior: First, society had convinced me that finding (or creating) romantic fairy-tale love would magically and instantly solve all my problems in life. Second, as long as I was engaged in either looking for the "right man" or being dramatically involved with one, I didn't have to pay proper attention to my own life.

As anyone who knows me knows, I've finally learned to look for the good in everything that happens in life. So it's no surprise that when I look back now at some of my most ridiculous and painful dating experiences, I can see the clever and essential gift that each one brought to my life.

When I was eighteen, I briefly dated a very narcissistic young man who had announced that I had to become his girlfriend because he loved the way I looked in a bathing suit. (Who could say no to that?) On our final date, he took me to an amusement park far away from home and told me that he wouldn't take me home until I convinced one of the game vendors to give me a giant stuffed animal for free, so that he could give the gigantic toy to his boss's son.

Now, before you get completely outraged, listen to this: That very same night, which was the last time I saw him, he also pointed out that he'd noticed my overly restrictive, calorie-counting eating behaviors. He told me that I had the same problem that his sister had, and that I needed help. He said I had to go see his sister's dietitian, and pulled the dietitian's card out of his wallet and handed it to me. I only saw the dietitian a couple of times, but she helped me so much and inspired me so much that I decided to change my major to Dietetics. I owe that guy a huge hug, if I ever see him again.

The musician who laughed at me when I told him I wanted to write and dance, who told me that I didn't have a creative bone in my body, made me so mad that I became determined to prove him wrong. I took my first dance class and published my first article right after I ended that relationship. Gracias, amigo!

One salsa partner, whom I was sure I would dance into old age with, abruptly danced off with someone else ten years younger. Luckily, before he took off he managed to complete his divine assignment for my life. For my birthday, he gave me what would prove to be a priceless gift: he took me to see my very first flamenco show. At the time, neither he nor I imagined that one day I'd become a professional flamenco dancer. And if he hadn't left me, I might never have left Vancouver and met Armando, the real love of my life.

The nuttiest part of each of my unfortunate relationships (and there were several more) is that afterwards I'd usually go through a phase where I thought I still wanted to be with the other person. This happened almost every time, no matter how miserable I'd actually been when I was with the guy.

I would obsessively focus on the good aspects of what I had lost, and somehow forget about all the horrible stuff (and there was usually more horrible stuff than good stuff). Through my own crazy logic, I'd convince myself that that horrible relationship was still better than no relationship. Also, I suspect that the romance novels that I used to read convinced me that glorious fairy-tale endings were always possible, no matter how warty the frog was.

I'm sharing this with you because I've observed similar patterns in many of my coaching clients, and in the people around me. From my very first coaching client, almost every single person I work with asks me for some kind of help with understanding and changing their relationship patterns.

Many clients have shared with me their experiences of emerging, bruised and disillusioned, from unfulfilling, half-committed relationships with partners who weren't anything even close to their vision of their ideal mate. In most cases, they'd given up on believing that a better kind of relationship could be possible for them, so they were willing to settle for much less than even second best.

Frequently, after a short period of time, the memory of their former partner's sins and fatal flaws would start to fade, and they would begin to attempt to resuscitate the relationship. Once again, I'd hear that infamous phrase: "I've decided I'm going to call him (or her), just this once, to try and finally get some closure."

I watched Jenna, a brilliant, beautiful, thirty-year-old nurse, continually try to reconnect with Benjamin, a man she'd met through an online dating service. Benjamin was a self-centered freeloader who loved to tell lovely, kind Jenna everything that was wrong with her. He was the one who ended the relationship.

Still, every time that Jenna started to feel lonely or bored, she'd be back online, messaging Ben "just this once," looking for that eternally evasive "closure." Every time she'd reconnect, he'd respond with something nice or funny, which would get her feelings revving again, only to eventually do something cruel that revealed, yet again, who he really was. At that moment, Jenna would remember her intense dislike for the "real" Ben, but then that knowledge would eventually fade away again to be replaced by the "but we used to have so much fun together" illusion.

Thankfully, these days Jenna finally understands that she deserves so much more from a man. Though she's still single, she's now completely focused on improving her own life, a life that has no room for men like Ben. And by focusing on what matters most in her own life, rather than distracting herself with dramatic entanglements with men who don't deserve her, Jenna has greatly improved her odds of attracting someone really wonderful.

Marcy, a forty-year-old advertising executive, contacted me when she was trying to recover from the end of her ten-year relationship with David, a personal trainer who was five years younger than her, and probably fifteen years younger emotionally. David had cheated on Marcy several times, and then had the audacity to break up with her. To most people, it would be clear that David was doing Marcy a favor, but Marcy felt more depressed every day, and couldn't get David out of her mind.

She obsessed about whether he was still seeing the latest woman, and spent most of her free time wondering if it would be better to email him or call him. Luckily, with a little help from me, she rarely did either.

As she focused on what she needed to do for her own life instead, Marcy grew more and more into her natural strength, beauty, and self-esteem. Just a few months after I met her, she radiated joy, enthusiasm, and success. And as for David? Recently, he'd begun to call, wanting desperately to reunite with her. From her new, more realistic perspective, Marcy couldn't believe she'd given him ten years of her life, and didn't plan on giving him another precious minute.

I've learned through my work around codependence that though it's fine to share my opinion if someone requests it, it's never appropriate to *tell* people what to do. Still, I do try to help my clients see and understand their own behaviors, to evaluate whether they're truly congruent with what they say that they want from life. If they can't detach from these painful relationships, I help them improve the choices that they make and the actions that they take by illuminating the fundamental conflict between their original description of how unfulfilling the old relationship was (i.e., "reality") and their optimistic attempts to reconnect with or resurrect it (i.e., "fantasy").

That's not to say that miracles can't happen. Bad people can sometimes become good people, and dramatic relationships can become dramatically more peaceful and healthy. Yet, in my experience, both partners need to undergo dramatic changes in order for that to happen, and need to be willing to truly see themselves, their lives, and their patterns, and be prepared to change them.

If you see yourself anywhere in these pages, I encourage you to feel optimistic, rather than discouraged. There is so much that you can do to get your life and your rational judgment back. When you learn and put into practice the fundamental principles of healthy self-care and healthy relationships, the love part takes care of itself.

In the next chapter, I'll discuss in detail some of the principles and techniques that have both transformed and healed my experience of relationships and life. I also have more good news. I, and many other people who've been on a similar journey, have discovered a miraculous truth: When you turn the spotlight of your life around and focus it on yourself, rather than focusing on what someone else is or isn't doing, many elements of your life begin to naturally shift.

When you finally stop trying so hard to manipulate and "fix" your relationships, they'll actually start to heal and transform on their own. One morning you'll wake up and realize that, whether you're in a relationship or not, you're really, truly happy. And thankfully, this won't be the fragile brand of happiness that depends on anyone else. That, my friend, is what makes for a real "happily ever after."

8

TEND TO YOUR OWN GARDEN—

LEAVE THEIR WEEDS ALONE

HEN I CAN, I ask audience members to tell me publicly or privately about the areas of their lives that concern them the most. Time and again, I'm amazed by how many people share the same issues. Here are some of the most common complaints that I hear, using quotes from different audience members:

> "As women, we're always so busy taking care of others that we forget about ourselves—I think that has happened to me."

> "I just feel such a high responsibility to look after others. It's my nature to be caring, to put everyone else first. I don't know any other way to be."

> "I don't take care of myself, but I constantly take care of everyone else."

As I write this, Armando and I have just made the difficult decision to move full-time to Canada (at least for now) because of all the things that are happening for me up north. Last year, I flew so often between Canada, the United States, and Mexico that it was starting to make me dizzy, and I never saw my husband for more than a handful of days at a stretch. There are also more opportunities for him in Canada than in Mexico.

His mother and three sisters actually took the news of the move surprisingly well. I'm so fortunate that this lovely, warm family has accepted and embraced me, and sometimes Armando even jokes that they love me more than they do him. Many foreigners who come along and "steal" away Latin sons (especially, as in my case, an only son) don't fare as well as I have.

That said, no Mexican son can move north without his family having something to say about it. The week before our move to Canada, one sister after another took me aside and, with worried eyes, said something like:

"Please take good care of my brother. We put him in your hands, we know that you love him very much and are so glad that he is with you. But *please*, take good care of him."

His oldest sister, Angelica, did this approximately once every day, and one time even called me into the kitchen "to talk" and then ambushed me with a traditional seed-throwing ceremony to ensure our abundance and success. Weeks later, I still occasionally found a wayward sesame seed when I washed my hair.

I was feeling more and more stressed by all this, until the moment came when we piled our suitcases in his sister Olimpia's car to go the airport. As I walked out the front door, Angelica pulled me to the side again.

"Susy, remember, we really need you to take care of our brother . . ."

That was it. I couldn't hold back any longer.

"Angelica, I'm sorry, but I have to say something. It was here, through this family, that I learned that people are responsible for themselves, that it's *not* a person's job to take care of everyone else. Armando is a very intelligent, capable man. *He can take care of himself!*"

Angelica raised her eyebrows and stepped back, and then her vivid features opened into a broad smile. She shook her head and laughed.

"I'm so sorry," she said, grasping my hands. "You're absolutely right. You're not his mother, but we've been treating you like you are. We just love our brother, and it's normal in our culture to act this way. We know he'll be just fine, really."

With a hug, we separated and I climbed into the waiting car. I had known that I could say this to her, and that she would get it. It is largely because of this wise, close-knit family that I am who I am today, and am qualified to write this chapter in this book.

CODEPENDENCE: COMPULSIVELY AVOIDING YOURSELF

A major turning point in my life arrived one day when, for the hundredth time, I called "Mama" Elvia (now my mother-in-law) to complain about her son. God bless her eternally, the woman is a saint. She'd already been listening patiently to me for a couple of years, as I'd call her whenever her son disappointed or frustrated me in some new way.

Mama Elvia finally interrupted me in the middle of my tirade and said something that she'd never said to me before: "Susy, I know it's been very difficult to put up with some of the things that

Armando does, and I'm not making excuses for anything that has happened, but I need to tell you this: You have to stop focusing on him and start focusing on your own life."

I was shocked into silence. Next, she recommended some books to read and told me to join a local group of Mexican women who supported each other in recovering their lives and healing from difficult relationships.

I read the books and went to the group, and there I discovered my core problem. This problem, which I now know to be the core issue of so many of my coaching clients and so many people in the world around me, was that my behavior fit the pattern of "codependence." This term was originally created to describe spouses and partners of alcoholics, when experts observed that these people exhibited common patterns of behavior.

Codependent behavioral patterns include: denying the true state of your life and how you feel about it; failing to recognize your own worth and legitimate needs; making the needs of others more important than your own; and attempting to control the behavior or well-being of others.

Apparently many different types of circumstances can cause a person to behave codependently, such as growing up in a stress- or anger-filled family, emotional or physical deprivation, and so on. To get into it all is beyond the scope of this book, but you should know that if you see yourself at all in the patterns that I've described, there are many highly effective steps that you can take to get yourself and your life back.

I learned two things in that group that changed my life forever: First, to save my own life, I needed to take my focus off of other people, and turn it back to myself. And second, I wouldn't be able to work this miracle by myself, so I would have to ask God, or a "higher power," for help. I finally saw that I had been using food, shopping, men, and drama to avoid facing myself and my true purpose in life.

WORRIED SICK—ABOUT EVERYONE ELSE

I see them everywhere. People, most commonly women, who have built their lives around the needs of others and have almost completely lost touch with who they really are. This goes far beyond being kind, generous, and helping others—I'm all for that. But when that behavior reaches the point where you're unable to meet your own most basic needs, and can't ever seem to pull back enough to take proper care of yourself, it's gone too far.

If this sounds like you, ask yourself this: Where is the motivation to help those around you truly coming from? Are you "helping" from a place of truly unconditional love, expecting no recognition and nothing in return, or do you take care of others because it's part of your public identity as a "good" person? Do you believe that if you help everyone around you it significantly reduces the probability that someone in your life will hurt, disappoint, or betray you?

Another question: Do you help others because you hope to change their behavior or control the circumstances in their lives? For example, if you're a parent, would you help your child pay for a professional university education but refuse to pay for art school, even if that was what they really wanted to study, on the grounds that you believe you know what's best for them? It's absolutely normal for a parent to want what they perceive to be best for their child, but that doesn't change the fact that in many cases they may end up doing more damage than good.

Finally, do you help others because it keeps you busy, busy, busy—so busy that at the end of your life, you'll have a noble, socially acceptable excuse for why you never lived your own dreams or never took proper care of your own health?

Many of us automatically "help" others, even though the recipient of our generosity may never actually have asked us for our assistance or input. In the extreme form, this can translate into a pattern of compulsively rescuing anyone around us who needs to be saved from something.

One of my coaching clients is financially very successful, and feels guilty about it. People sense this, and constantly approach him, asking to borrow money. Because of his own good fortune and innate generosity, he usually says yes. Unfortunately, the money doesn't usually help the borrower's long-term situation, as they typically don't change their financial behaviors and so eventually end up in trouble again. The borrower then resents the fact that they owe my client (even if my client has told them to forget the debt), and the relationship is tainted forever.

Another person comes along and asks for money, and my client comes to the rescue once again (or at least he used to). The same thing happens again—and again. He can't understand how this person whom he helped "save" could now resent him and even badmouth him to others.

When we do things compulsively, it's like we've gone insane in that area of our lives, and are unable to see that the same behavior always produces the same result. "But how could they do that?" we cry. They do, and they did, and they will again. Some things just don't change, unless you do.

When we compulsively help, we assume that we know what's best for others. We believe, sometimes quite rightly, that if we don't help the people around us, their lives will descend into chaos and disaster.

What we don't realize is that often the greatest gift that we can give to others is to allow their actions, or inaction, to lead to the natural consequences, which may indeed be chaos and disaster. Sometimes, by taking care of people too much, we block them from the very events that would bring necessary change and growth into their lives.

TEND TO YOUR OWN GARDEN

The people in our lives are so essential to our health and happiness. And not just the ones we care about most. As I love to point out, studies repeatedly show that people who have more social contacts overall enjoy better physical and mental health. It's not just the interactions with your spouse or best friend that count and add richness to your life; taking the time to chat with the corner grocery clerk or stopping to say hi to a neighbor can make a significant difference to your wellness and quality of life.

Most of us who live in cities have forgotten the lost art of neighborhood friendliness. If you're feeling tired and stressed, one of the easiest ways to get yourself out of a funk is by taking the time to smile and say a few words to the people you encounter throughout your day.

I spent the majority of the last few years in resort towns in Mexico, and fell in love with the typical Mexican kindness and hospitality that I experienced every day that I lived there. I had been a city girl all my life, and discovered that I loved the welcoming feel of a small town. Unfortunately, I also soon discovered its dark side: the slippery slope of small-town gossip.

One morning, I ran into a friend while grocery shopping. Rita came over as soon as she saw me. She had an uncharacteristic look of concern on her face.

"How are you, Susan? Is everything okay?"

I didn't know what she was talking about.

"What do you mean?" I asked.

"Well, er. . ." she looked uncomfortable.

"What? Tell me what's going on," I urged her.

"Well, it's just that Betty said something to me the other day that I just couldn't believe," she said. "You see . . . she told me she read on the Internet that you had gotten really depressed and had had a nervous breakdown, and that they wouldn't let you work as a doctor anymore. She said that's why you had to leave and move to Mexico."

For a moment my mouth just hung open. And then I started to laugh. Rita watched me nervously; she was probably afraid that I was having another "breakdown."

"Rita," I continued to laugh. "It sounds like Betty's been spending time on my website. I speak and write really openly about my experiences with depression, because it's one of the things that I educate people about. My depression occurred at a time in my life when I wasn't being true to myself, and ever since I started living a more authentic, balanced life, I've been just fine. Mexico has been a big part of that authentic life, but I *still* have my license and work as a doctor in Canada. You know that! So don't worry about me, I'm okay."

We never talked about it again. Thinking about it later, I felt somewhat shocked and sad. I'm used to being misunderstood and didn't really care that someone would jump to those kinds of erroneous conclusions about me. But the fact that someone would deliberately share their own conclusions with others made me more than a little uncomfortable.

How much time do you spend thinking about, judging, complaining about, or discussing what other people are doing? How many people that you regularly spend time with spend their time gossiping about others? What if right now you made the decision to change the subject any time someone started telling an unkind story about someone else?

Now, an even more important question: How much of your day do you spend looking at your own life, what you're doing and not doing, and what *you* need to change?

I won't let my coaching clients waste precious minutes of their session going on and on about the terrible things that the other people in their lives are doing. All I need is a basic understanding of the situation—after that, say no more. Going on and on in great detail about what's wrong with the behavior of others can be a highly effective way to avoid truly productive conversation. You avoid discussing the changes you could make in the only areas that you actually have control over: your own actions, reactions, and choices.

My friend Marla is struggling with a very difficult home situation. Her husband yells too much, flirts too much, and spends his money on expensive toys, rather than supporting his family. I feel bad for my friend, and make the time to listen to her, but there's usually a point in the conversation where I have to interrupt and change the subject. If I don't, she'll just keep talking about Joe's latest exploits. I want to hear about *her*, not the twenty most offensive things that Joe's been up to in the last week.

It's important to have people to confide in, people that you can cry with and yell with, people you know will listen. But there comes a point when complaining about others and describing yet another way in which you've been made a victim just isn't helpful at all. Marla's complaining might help release some of her stress and frustration in the short term, but in the long term it doesn't change a thing.

Marla is a hilarious and generous woman. She's highly creative, loves to have fun, and has two wonderful kids. Imagine two conversations: In the first, Marla spends an hour crying about Joe's latest exploits; in the second, she relates how Georgie, her youngest, pulled an April Fool's hoax on his first grade class, and then talks about her dream of opening a pottery workshop.

I'd like you to consider how Marla's body would experience each of these two types of conversations. It may be an obvious question, but which conversation do you think would promote better health for her? Finally, which of the two conversations do you think would be likely to produce positive emotions and outcomes in Marla's life?

There was a time when drama and conversations about drama used to dominate my life. Most of my conversations and thoughts revolved around self-righteousness, victimization, and complaining both to and about others. Not surprisingly, my career and dreams for my life almost slowed to a halt during that time. In fact, I was so busy feeling sorry for myself and complaining about others that I pretty much forgot my dreams.

In the last couple of years, I've finally enjoyed an amazing trajectory and series of events, in both my professional and personal life. I've gotten married; my speaking career is thriving; I finally have a publisher for this book—something I've talked about for almost seven years; I'm back on TV with my own show in the works; and I'm still amazed by the opportunities and experiences I've had as a dancer and performer.

I've been able to do all this because my life is finally emotionally healthy. And if it's not *completely* emotionally healthy yet (I'm not going to lie to you!), at least it's much, much better. I still love others and help them as much as I can, but my life is now about what I *can* do, not what others are or are not doing.

The Serenity Prayer from the twelve-step programs says it so well:

> *God, grant me the serenity to accept the things that I cannot change, the courage to change the things I can, and the wisdom to know the difference.*

The next time you catch yourself complaining about someone, feeling sorry for yourself, or wishing that someone else would finally act in the way that you want them to—stop. Stop right there, and ask yourself: What do I need to do right now to look after myself and my life? Maybe there's a pile of unopened bills on the table that needs your attention. Maybe it's time that you laced up your sneakers and started that daily walk habit you've talked about for years. Maybe you need to pull out a journal and start writing in it. There's always something much more important for you to do than waste another minute of your life complaining about, or focusing on, something (or someone) that you have no control over.

Tend to your own garden and watch the deliciously scented blossoms emerge and fill in that previously scraggly, weedy space. Their beauty and perfection will amaze you.

OWN YOUR OWN BUTTONS

Even if all your relationships are humming along fairly smoothly, you're still going to run into rough spots. Some people claim never to get ruffled or phased by anything. I'm not calling their personal serenity into question, I just don't think that I will achieve that kind of steady state in this lifetime. Odds are, neither will you.

However, even though you still might occasionally *react* to something that happens in your life (particularly when the person you love most in the world knows *exactly* what to say or do to set you off), you can still dramatically change the experience and expression of that reaction. I call this "owning your own buttons."

Lucia, the feisty *señora* who owned an apartment that I rented in Cabo, has been married to her husband Marcos for several decades, and she once shared one of her trade secrets with me over a glass of icy sweet *Jamaica* tea.

"Never, ever let them know that something bugs you," she whispered, out of earshot of Marcos, who was sitting outside on the deck. "When you get married and your husband does some-thing that drives you crazy, like leaving his dirty socks on the floor, *never let him know that it drives you bananas!*"

I didn't really get it. "But won't I want him to pick up his dirty socks?" I asked.

"Of course!" she laughed. "But you can't let him know how much it bothers you. If you do, the day that you get in an argu-ment, he'll know just how to get to you—he'll throw his dirty socks all over your home, just to bug you, and you'll go *wild* with fury! Trust me, it's better that he doesn't know."

It was rather bizarre but sage advice. Unfortunately, I'm not very good at concealing my opinions, and Armando, as a result, knows exactly what to do to get my goat. To be fair, though, Armando's much more of a neat freak than I am, which makes me far more likely to be the one using socks as a secret weapon.

We've all got those touchy points that shoot us from mildly riled to stratospheric. Whenever Armando and I get into a "heated dis-cussion," he's usually the first to accuse me of raising my voice. Of course, he'll usually do that in a tone that's far from quiet.

"Please stop yelling at me," he'll say loudly, interrupting me. Now, I've got a fairly strong voice, particularly when I'm being wronged or falsely accused, and believe me, I can yell with the very best of them. For that reason, I'm usually extremely confident of the fact that, at that moment, *I'm not yelling.*

That said, when I'm already getting testy and someone accuses me of yelling—*when I'm not*—it's virtually guaranteed to increase my decibel level. At which point, I really am yelling about the fact that I most definitely wasn't yelling before. At those moments, I'd hate to imagine where my blood pressure would register, on the scale between "asleep" and "high risk of stroke."

Research has demonstrated that couples that become negative or hostile when discussing problems experience negative effects on their immune system that can last up to twenty-four hours, even if they've long since kissed and made up! Another study showed that people who experienced frequent negative personal interactions with the people who were closest to them were significantly more likely to experience chest pain, heart attacks, and even death. Men who frequently experience feelings of intense hostility and anger have been shown to be at greater risk of developing hypertension, heart disease, and diabetes.

A close friend of mine once shared with me the sad story of her first marriage. Emily and her husband Darren were both hot-tempered and opinionated, and their disagreements often escalated into shouting contests. She confessed to me that whenever she got so angry with him that she simply couldn't contain her rage any-more, she'd end the conversation with the words, "I wish you'd just drop dead!" and would storm off. One day, the morning after another one of their arguments, he did just that. Darren died of a heart attack.

You can learn to control your reactions and the quality of your discussions with others. Start by simply developing an awareness of your problem spots or "hot buttons." Lately, I've noticed that most of my arguments with Armando happen while we're in the car, when I'm driving. I'll get annoyed by something that happens on the road, or something happens that makes us run late, and the next thing I know, we're arguing. It's clear to me that in this case, I am the problem. He'll usually say something to me that magnifies my bad mood, but I usually start it through my childish reaction to whatever's going on. The next time I get into the car with him, I'm going to do all I can to let any petty roadway irritants and annoyances just slide right off my skin.

How will I do that? First, I know that when I haven't eaten enough, I get grumpy more quickly. So, before getting into the car I'll make sure that I eat something substantial. I also know that I get really irritable if I'm under pressure or feel rushed, so I'll try to leave with enough time to get to the destination. Finally, if I feel my temper starting to soar when something happens, I'll resort to deep breathing and keep my mouth shut. I'll turn on the radio and look for a song that I like to break the mood. Perhaps I'll ask Armando something about his day.

Note that none of these solutions has anything to do with changing Armando's behavior. Sure, I'd rather that he not make snide comments whenever my cranky alter ego comes out, but I can't do anything about what he does—other than changing what I do first.

Even though at first you might not be able to catch your reaction before it gets going, start to pay attention to how it feels. What's the first sign that you're about to explode? Do your shoulders and neck start to tense and creep up? Do you grit your teeth? Does your brain start boiling like a teakettle that's about to sound off?

The next time you feel yourself starting to react, see if you can interrupt your reaction. Here are some things you can try:

> *Do something unexpected*
The next time someone starts to push your buttons, try to break the mood by doing something funny, kind, or loving. If it's your romantic partner, stop and give them a surprise hug and kiss—and make sure you pack it full of love. Or take your pent-up energy and do a silly little dance of frustration that's sure to make both of you laugh. Once tempers have calmed down, you might suggest revisiting and resolving the issue later, at a better time.

> *Take a time-out*
As I'm most likely to be the mercurial one in any argument (what can I say, I'm a flamenco dancer), I've learned that often

the only way to prevent doing or saying something that I'll regret is to remove myself from the situation. If I start getting really angry, or the conversation is getting potentially hurtful, I'll often just calmly say that I don't want to participate in this type of discussion, and excuse myself and go to another room.

I don't make it about the other person; rather, I just say that it would be best if I take a time-out. Once I've calmed down, I will return, and if I'm capable of it I'll put a smile on my face. If I need to, I'll "tend to my own garden" for a while by doing something that needs to be done (like the dishes). It makes me feel better, I calm down, and I also manage to get something constructive done in the process. Later, I'll find a good time to bring up the problem, and look at it from a fresh perspective. Often we find that what seemed like a big deal at the time just isn't anymore.

❧ Observe the present moment

I'm not a big fan of meditation per se (I find I get bored way too quickly), but one concept that I do borrow from the Zen crowd is the concept of "mindfulness." According to this tradition, whenever you engage in something, you should do it mindfully. In our culture, we spend so much time in our heads—worrying, planning, and going over to-do lists—that we go through our day completely disconnected from the rich texture of our lives and our bodies.

Take note the next time you take a shower in the morning: Where's your mind? Is it in or outside of your body? Are you thinking about the rest of your day or about something that happened the day before? To switch into a "mindful" shower mode, get out of your head and back into your body by enjoying the heat of the water as it hits your body. Savor the fresh scent and the feeling of your soap and shampoo lather in your hands. Enjoy the soft warmth of your towel afterwards, as you dry off.

Later, when you're about to get angry, you can flex this new "mindfulness" muscle to help you move out of the confrontation and into the world around you. Perhaps you can notice the song of a bird outside and tune in to it for a moment. Maybe there's a beautiful bouquet of flowers sitting on the table just off to your left. Take a moment to really *see* the lustrous, satiny petals of those tulips. Sometimes when you allow yourself just a few seconds to disconnect from the drama and reconnect with your surroundings, it breaks the tension and short-circuits the entire button reaction. The other person won't even know that you're doing it.

Now, I have to emphasize here that whether you decide to control your reactions by taking a time-out, hugging the other person, or focusing for an instant on the beautiful view out the window, it's most effective if you keep what you're doing to yourself. When we deliberately change our reactions or the way we handle difficult situations, it can occasionally be tempting to say something like this:

"If you're going to be this immature, I'm going to go off and tend to *my* garden for a change—I think I've wasted enough precious moments of my life on your #@%$# weeds!"

Not only will they wonder what the heck you're talking about, it'll also seriously undermine your chances of ever improving your relationship.

It's equally ineffective to say: "You're on your own now, buddy! Dr. Biali says it's absolutely impossible for me to get you to change your rotten behavior. I'm the only hope we have, so I'm going to look after my own life! I hope you hit bottom, because you really deserve it!"

Whenever you detach from a difficult situation with another person, do it kindly, gently, and with love. Believe me, I know that's not always easy. Let people experience the natural consequences of their actions and reactions. And, in the same process, take back control of your own.

LEARN TO BE HAPPY, NO MATTER WHAT THEY DO

As I mentioned earlier, I don't ever expect to attain a permanent state of unflappable serenity. You might feel the same. At any moment, some person (and possibly someone you haven't even met yet) may suddenly hold the potential to ruin your hour, if not your entire day. Have you had the experience of being in a perfectly good mood, happily going about your business, when someone suddenly barges in and turns your mood upside down?

If you don't take personal responsibility for the state of your moods and happiness, you'll end up feeling like a ball in a pinball machine. Everything will start out straight and smooth, and then someone will hit you unexpectedly from the left and make you feel guilty or sad. Next, someone else comes along and hits you from the right, making you feel angry or irritable. Bang! Ping! Wham! You never know where the next hit's going to come from.

From now on, resolve to only be infected by the good moods of people around you. If someone is feeling joyful or enthusiastic, delight in them, let the feeling in, and let it lift you up. But if someone walks into your day exuding anger, pessimism, gloom, or is looking for a fight, don't let yourself get sucked in or dragged down. Especially if they deliberately try to take you down with them, because they will!

It's a beautiful thing, and so freeing, to decide to be happy no matter what they do. If your spouse is late for dinner and never called to let you know, enjoy the delicious stew that you cooked for the two of you, instead of stewing over his or her irresponsibility. Someone may as well enjoy your fabulous food, and who's more deserving of that than you?

If someone lets you down, don't let it wreck your day. If someone deliberately does something that usually makes you go wild with frustration, choose to make this time different. Remember that in many situations the most constructive, helpful thing you can do is to calmly turn your attention to whatever needs tending in your own life.

Also, remember that when you do take care of your own needs, and stop trying to do everything for others, everyone usually wins in the end—no matter how challenging the initial transition or how strong their (and your) initial resistance to change.

People are hard enough to interact with at the very best of times. To enjoy the people in your life to the fullest, train yourself to minimize the impact that the negative stuff has on your mood, your health, your relationships, and your life. Guard and conserve your precious time and energy—you've simply got too many other wonderful things to do, to enjoy, and to be!

5

GET A
LIFE!

9

DARE TO DREAM

I GRABBED MY SMALL, soggy towel and wiped away the sweat that stung my eyes. Outside, a car drove slowly past, kicking up a cloud of desert dust. The driver peered into the little laundry room, curious about the loud Spanish music that poured out through the grimy window.

That September, the hottest month of the year in the dry desert town of Cabo San Lucas, I had lost my dance studio, had been rejected by the only flamenco group in town, and didn't have a single gig. All I had was the unimaginable heat of that tiny room, and a small beat-up CD player. I danced for hours as the laundry machines pumped hot fumes into the suffocating space.

It's incredible to me now, how tenaciously I hung on to my vision of performing flamenco in Mexico, despite the seemingly endless parade of obstacles that kept popping up. Every time I tried to grab an opportunity, it seemed to disintegrate in my hands.

Determined to come up with some kind of a viable show, I

sought out guitarists and other musicians. At one particularly desperate moment, I even tried to collaborate with a bongo player! While we were in Puerto Vallarta, Armando, wanting to do anything he could to help me live my dream, went door to door to restaurants and anywhere else he thought musicians might hang out, asking about flamenco guitarists. He actually unearthed a couple: one proved to be unable to play flamenco, though he tried hard, and the other knew how to play but could never remember any details of what we'd already rehearsed.

After so many failures, I started to wonder if *I* was the problem—after all, I was the common denominator in every situation. Armando kept telling me I just needed to do my own show, with CD music if I had to, but I was stuck in what I knew: live flamenco, with live musicians. For almost two years, I refused to believe that people might actually pay me to dance all by myself.

In Vallarta, at Armando's urging, I convinced a few hotel and restaurant owners to give me a chance to audition, only to learn that unpaid "auditions" were actually this country's favorite way to get free entertainment for their guests and clients. By the time I'd reached Cabo and had exhausted all the options I'd been able to find there, I was close to giving up.

Everyone thought I was nuts—why eke out an existence in the desert when I could enjoy a doctor's income if I just went home? But I couldn't do that. It would have meant abandoning my very soul. I kept practicing in that laundry room.

A month later, my phone still hadn't rung—not even once. Armando was starting to get nervous. At that point, I wasn't working at all as a doctor anymore, as I wanted to "give this dance thing a real chance." It wasn't looking good. I remember sitting on the couch with him one night, crying about how badly it all still seemed to be going.

"You know, maybe you should start to think about working more in Canada again," he started.

I shot up onto my feet, my tears immediately turning to rage. "What!? What are you saying?"

He looked up at me with sad eyes. "*Amor*, you know how much I believe in you. But maybe you should just face it. You don't have one single gig yet. Not one."

I stormed off to the bedroom and sat on the edge of the bed, cradling my face in my hands. I was not going to give up. I was *not* going to give up! The next day, I went right back to practicing in the laundry room.

A few days later, the phone rang. It was the PR director of one of the best resort hotels on the planet. The hotel's general manager, who had just been recognized in Cannes as one of the top hoteliers in the world, wanted to meet with me to discuss plans for the most important week of the year: Christmas and New Year's.

On Christmas Eve, just three months after those scorching laundry room rehearsals, a small wooden stage awaited me—in front of the hotel's sumptuous open-air restaurant. Behind the stage, a blazing bonfire shot sparks up into the cool desert night.

Minutes before I went out the doors to start the show, Ricardo, one of the guitarists, pulled me aside.

"Susy," he whispered urgently. "There's something we think you should know."

My heart stopped. What was wrong?

"Just in case it might catch you off guard," he continued, "we thought we should tell you that Sean Penn is having dinner out there, right in front of your stage. We wanted you to be prepared—don't let it throw you off!"

That was a wise move on Ricardo's part—I probably would have fallen over or tripped while dancing if they hadn't warned me.

As I stepped onto the stage, Ricardo de Luna and his brother Raul, my two newest friends who also happen to be world-class guitarists with a long list of successful albums, strummed the opening chords of a hauntingly beautiful melody. I began to dance.

As I turned and swirled my skirts in the moonlight, listening to the guitars and the waves crashing on the nearby sand, I gloried in knowing that I was finally exactly where I was supposed to be, and that every single moment of my suffering and self-doubt had been worth it.

After the show, I asked the de Lunas who the loud people at the very back of the restaurant were, the ones who stood, cheering and waving small lights in the air after each performance.

"Oh, them—those are the owners of the Los Angeles Lakers. They really liked you!"

I'm still amazed by all the things that have happened since those hot, desperate days of dancing in the laundry room. I've only been able to share a sliver of it all with you here. Looking back, I can see that it all really did unfold perfectly over time and turn out for the best, even though for several years everything seemed to be going wrong. I think life often tests us like that to see how much we really want something. Our passion, devotion, and persistence get tested over and over again, until one day our faith and efforts finally pay off.

The day I met Ricardo and Raul, they gave me a copy of one of their CDs so that I could familiarize myself with their work. When I got home from that first meeting, the first thing I did was pop their CD into my beat-up player. As it started to play, I had to grab the nearest chair and sit down. The first song I had selected turned out to be one that I'd made a copy of long ago. I had no idea that it had been recorded by Guitarras de Luna. Without knowing it, I had been listening to their music for years.

The beautiful guitar music that came out of my speakers was one of my favorite songs. That hot September in the laundry room, I'd rehearsed to that song for hours. I never imagined that I'd shortly meet, perform with, and become close friends with the very artists who arranged and recorded it. The whole time I was in that hot, sweaty little laundry "studio," *they* were rehearsing, too, just fifteen miles down the highway from me.

For years, it seemed that my dream was just that—a silly dream. By the time I was dancing in that stifling laundry room, I was thirty-five years old, and it had only been three years since I'd started studying flamenco. I hadn't taken regular classes in almost two years, other than a trip to Spain to study at the International Flamenco Festival in Jerez. It would have made plenty of logical sense to give up, but I just couldn't.

When my break finally came, those relentless obstacles that had popped up every time I tried a new approach, that shot down every attempt I made before I even got myself off the ground, suddenly disappeared.

The reason I'm so passionate about sharing my story with you is that I hope to inspire you to follow whatever dream you hold in your heart. Chances are that you think that you're probably not good enough, or that it's just too late. Well let me tell you this: Whether or not you're "good enough," by someone else's or your own standards, really doesn't matter. It's what your heart is asking you to do that counts and holds all your future miracles. You see, *I'm not a great dancer.* Not even close.

I dance with passion, I love to be on stage, I love the music and the movements, and I love to connect with an audience. But compared to most others who earn a living dancing, I've barely had any training. And for most of my time in Cabo, I didn't even have a mirror to rehearse in front of!

If I had taken dance classes since I was a little girl, God's miracle wouldn't be so impressive. If I were a flamenco prodigy who'd spent several years training full-time in Spain, it all might be a little more understandable. If I had had a real flamenco mentor or teacher during those years in Mexico, that might have helped, too. If I'd been rich, and could have lived off my savings to indulge my dance whims, that also would have made things easier, and less risky. I came to Mexico without any savings, still trying to pay off what was left of my student loans.

All I had was a little bit of talent, a lot of passion, a big dream, and piles of faith. I suspect that you, too, have access to each of these four things. They're all that you need.

YOUR DREAMS ARE THE ROADMAP
OF YOUR SOUL

Each of us is absolutely unique. I see it every day in my coaching work. When I ask someone about their dream for their life, I've never gotten the same answer twice.

If I ask someone what their dream is, and they say that they don't have one, or don't have any idea what it might be, I'll often have them do a powerful exercise. I ask them to take out a blank sheet of paper and write down a vivid description of a day in their most wonderful, ideal life. Why not take your journal out right now and do this exercise? You'll also find it in the free download-able workbook that accompanies this book. (If you haven't already done so, you can get it at www.susanbiali.com/workbook.html.)

When you wake up on your ideal day, where are you? What do your surroundings look like? Who is with you? What does this day feel like? What do you do, and who do you see and interact with? How do you earn your living?

I adapted this exercise from one that I found years ago as part of the twelve-week program in Julia Cameron's brilliant book, *The Artist's Way*. I'll talk more about Cameron's work in Chapter 10. Right now, let me tell you how doing this exercise impacted my life.

When I first worked through Cameron's course, I'd only been working for a year as a full-time doctor in walk-in clinics, and had started to take my very first dance classes. Though the dancing helped, I found the clinic work to be stressful, and was dismayed to discover that I didn't really enjoy it.

Whenever I had a free morning, I'd trudge through the rain to my favorite Italian café a couple of blocks away. There, I'd sip hot tea from a hand-painted Italian cup, eat a rich Italian cookie, pretend I was in Italy, and write in my journal, dreaming about a more fulfilling life.

It was also there that I read and wrote my way through Cameron's book, and wrote my first description of a day in my ideal life. I still have the notebook that I used.

That imaginary day, my ideal day, I woke up in a sun-filled ocean-side villa in Italy, next to my gorgeous Italian husband. We'd have breakfast together on our terrace, and then he'd head off to work. A busy author and public figure, I'd spend the morning doing media interviews and other administrative tasks. For lunch, I'd join a friend at a lovely outdoor café, before returning home to the villa to settle into my writing (my most recent book) for the afternoon. In the evening, my sexy husband would come home, and we'd go out for dinner and then dancing.

Fast forward to last year, eight years after I described that ideal day in my notebook: I woke up in a beachside villa, next to my sexy Mexican husband. We were in Mexico, not Italy, and we didn't actually own the villa, but we'd been living in it for over a year. I spent my free time handling media publicity and writing, just as I'd imagined, and frequently lunched with friends in charming outdoor restaurants overlooking the water. Armando and I did go out dancing at night—though I had never imagined that we'd be paid for it!

Despite what you might think after hearing this story, I don't really agree with today's popular emphasis on "manifesting" and "attracting." For those who aren't familiar with this, I'm referring to the idea that a person can create or attract anything that they want in life, through the force of their own will. I'm not disputing the importance of having a vision for your life or setting clear goals. I also agree that certain behaviors, such as kindness and generosity, do seem to "attract" the same to your life. Yet during a time in my life when I studied the techniques and theories of manifestation and attraction and enthusiastically applied them to almost everything, I found that I lost touch with my soul and the true purpose of my life. I've found, and observed in others, that when we focus too much on being the "creator," or even "co-creator" in our lives, it's both easy and tempting to view life as a giant gumball dispenser that gives you whatever you want. And just like those fairytales in which the hero is given three wishes, our more selfish "manifestations" tend to backfire in typical "be careful what you wish for" style. At least that's been my experience.

I do believe that by acknowledging to yourself, vividly, what your dream life would look and feel like, you become open to noticing related opportunities that arise, and begin to make choices that lead you towards that life. I have also found that praying for guidance and asking for the best outcome for any particular situation (without insisting on the terms of that outcome) can be very helpful. Whether or not you're personally or cosmically "creating" or "attracting" the positive events that arise doesn't even really matter.

Simply recognizing your dream can be a huge first step towards opening up to its possibility in your life. Acknowledging what you truly want may also be the first time that you allow yourself to believe that you might be allowed to have a life that you enjoy and feel fulfilled by.

Reviewing this exercise with clients has convinced me that we all come with a very unique God-given blueprint for our lives. When asked, we may automatically say that we just want a nice house, a nice car, 2.5 kids, and a job with great benefits (and that may really be the dream for many people), but I'm always amazed by what people come up with when I push them a little.

Here are some examples of dreams that I unearthed in some of my clients (some details, as always, have been changed to protect their identities): a nanny who wants to build a specialty store on eBay; a former CEO who wants to own her own resort retreat; a health practitioner who loves designing "spa" bathrooms; a financial advisor who sees herself speaking internationally about mental health; a sales executive who is secretly developing a new invention; a corporate manager who fantasizes about living on a dude ranch; and a fireman who wants to become a poet. The dreams I hear from people are consistently surprising and original, yet they often come out of the mouths of people who describe themselves as "past their prime" and "boring." I call that ridiculous!

By the way, having a dream doesn't necessarily mean you have to change your life, or career, or location. I talked to another expert coach the other day who told me that she worries when she observes people with "everyday" jobs feeling pressured by all this "passion" talk to find work that they're more passionate about. The problem in those situations is that the pressure's coming from outside, not inside. I encourage you to go with how you feel. If you're honest with yourself, you'll know what you want to change. It may be very little or it may be everything.

I love sharing the story of my client Joanie, who called me one summer day after seeing me talk about life and dreams on TV.

"I'm not sure if you can help me, and I'm not sure what I need help with, but I do know that I'd really like you to be my coach. Would you work with me?" she asked.

We had our first session that week and she told me her story. She was forty-five, and for the last twenty years raising her four children had been her full-time job. Now that the last one was out of the house, she didn't know what to do.

"I want to do something with my life," she told me, "but I really have no idea what. I worked as a waitress for a few years after I got out of school, but didn't really like it. I only have a high school education, and I'm not really good at anything, other than being a mom."

I get really excited when I hear words like that, as I just know that something big, and fabulous, is usually lurking right under the "I'm not good at anything" surface.

We spoke for over an hour and I pushed and poked at Joanie with one question after another, from every angle I could think of, to get her to start dreaming again. We discovered that though she hadn't taken a trip in years, she would love to travel to Europe. She also suddenly remembered that she had loved to draw as a child, and had delighted in sewing adorable outfits for her children when they were young. In her spare time, she loved to browse through clothes at beautiful boutiques. For her, visiting a designer store was like spending the afternoon in a world-class museum, without having to pay admission!

When we had our second session a few weeks later, I encountered a completely different Joanie. The first time we'd spoken she was quiet and unsure of herself. This time, she was so full of energy and overflowing with ideas that I could barely keep up with her.

"I'm going to Milan!" she announced. "I found a fashion design course that's just perfect for me, and I'm going to go!" I clutched the phone, and felt my mouth fall open as she continued.

"I'm going to be a children's fashion designer," she said. "When I used to make clothes for my kids, tons of people asked me to make clothes for their kids, too. I didn't have time then, but I do now. I'm so excited!"

That was a few months ago. After her highly successful dream trip to Milan, Joanie has come up with a name for her new business, is working on her website, and already has her first clients. She has so many ideas and steps in her elaborate business plan that sometimes she doesn't know what to do first. She sends me emails, telling me that she feels alive, joyful, purposeful, and occasionally totally terrified. She loves her life.

I didn't really do anything, other than not accept her answer when she told me that she didn't have any true talents or dreams. I also torpedoed every excuse she gave me, how she was too late, too old, too scared, not talented enough, not educated enough, not brave enough, and many others.

Sometimes when I encourage a client to dream, what eventually emerges from their mouth and heart doesn't have anything to do with what they're doing right now in their life. If that sounds like you, it doesn't mean that you have to abandon what you're doing right now. For now, you might even be able to keep your "day job," or much of your life, as is, and still begin your dream, or some form of it. I did that, as a doctor by day, dancer by night, for several years—until I was ready and the time was right.

The "day in your dream life" exercise, and any other dreams you might have, give you clues to what you need to start doing or exploring in your free time, right now. So, ask yourself: What could you do, right now, on the side, to start pointing your life towards your true "North Star"—the place in life where you'd ultimately love to be?

DON'T GIVE UP BEFORE THE MIRACLE

Just before the tide changes, it may seem like your dream will never come true. I had read enough inspirational books to know that, almost universally, success lies on the other side of failure. If I hadn't had that knowledge to hang on to, I might have caved before my dream finally came true.

Protect your dreams very carefully. Fortify them with the stories of other people who have made their dreams happen, especially those whose dreams are similar to your own. What did they do to succeed? What kind of challenges did they face? How long did it take them? What advice do they give to others now?

Seek out mentors. Ask people who have lived the experiences that you would love to have how they got there. In my case, I didn't know anyone personally who was living a model for the kind of life that I dreamed of, so I sought out books written by people who were living their dreams.

Fill up your head and heart with the stories and words of others to hang on to when times get tough. Protect your precious dreams: choose very carefully who you tell. There are people I love whom I won't hang out with when I'm incubating a new project or leap of faith, because they're just too full of fear and stories of why things in life don't work. When I'm gathering my courage to take my next big risk, I can't afford to let any negativity in.

If you have that burning belief in your heart, a knowledge that you can create, experience, or be something very special, hold tightly to it and hug it for warmth when the world outside starts to feel cold and scary. Even if there isn't another soul in the world who encourages you, don't let it go.

If you ever get to the point where you feel alone, are almost ready to give up, and perhaps just a need a word or two of encouragement, don't hesitate to go to my website, www.susanbiali.com, and send me a message or email. I won't laugh at your dream, I promise, and maybe I'll even be able to help you or give you the strength to take one more step.

I believe that we are born with the dreams that we have in our hearts, and we wouldn't be given them without having the ability to walk that path. There's always a reason for our dreams. More often than not, when we take steps towards them, we end up somewhere that we never even imagined going, we experience lessons and joys so profound that we could never have come up with them in our own imaginations. So, as important as it is to take steps in your life that honor the fulfillment of a dream, talent, or longing that you have in your soul, I think it's just as important to let that dream take you where it wants to go.

As you may have noticed, when I first wrote about my ideal day, I didn't mention anything about dancing flamenco. At the time I was learning to dance salsa, but I didn't even really know what flamenco was. I also never imagined that my sexy Latin husband might also be a dance instructor, and that we would teach salsa professionally. As for our celebrity students—I wouldn't have dreamed up that one in a million years! I just dreamed of living in a beautiful warm place with a beautiful warm man, with enough time to write and dance and enjoy life. And when I first started to imagine it, I didn't think that I would actually ever live it, as it seemed so far away from my everyday life.

Hang in there. Get through one more day. Take one more small risk. Don't be afraid if it doesn't make any sense to anyone—in fact, it may not even make sense to *you*. In my experience, the latter is a particularly good sign!

Listen to that "crazy" dream in your heart. Take the next tiny step towards it, whatever that may be. Step by courageous step, you'll live your way into the life of your dreams, accompanied by a waterfall of miracles that will blow your mind.

Believe in your dreams. The more improbable they seem, the more likely they will come to fruition, or lead you down an unimaginably delicious, surprise-laden path. And regardless of whether your original dreams ever come true, I assure you that in the end, the journey itself will bring you more joy and fulfillment than you could ever imagine.

10

HEAL YOUR LIFE THROUGH
CREATIVITY

*I*N HER BOOK *Walking in this World: The Practical Art of Creativity,* Julia Cameron points out that "when we avoid our creativity, we avoid ourselves." When you deliberately get in touch with your natural sense of play and creativity, you begin to uncover long-forgotten aspects of yourself, along with new joys and talents that you never knew existed. This playful journey of discovery connects you to feelings, abilities, and experiences so rich and delightful that at some moments you'll laugh or shout out loud with the sheer joy of it.

Where do you stand in your relationship between your practical self and your creative self? They're not actually two different "selves," but we typically see it that way. There's the practical person who needs to go to work and put food on the table, and then the dreaming child inside who longs for an entire afternoon spent finger-painting.

Obviously, the practical self needs to be in charge of our life, or else we'd starve, right? Not necessarily. It depends on how you define starvation.

Four years ago, I left behind a steady income in one of the world's most beautiful cities to live in a one-room apartment with no air conditioner overlooking the sea in Bucerias, Mexico, a small ramshackle village just north of Puerto Vallarta. I've already mentioned the cockroaches that came along with the latter (not to mention giant airborne locusts and the biggest flying ants I've ever seen), so I won't belabor that aspect of the experience.

For most of my life, my creative self was starving. After my post-residency epiphany, things were significantly better, but she still felt like she was being maintained on a spare, inadequate diet. I found pockets of time to take dance classes and to meet my freelance article deadlines, but I still felt forced to take on as much medical work as possible in order to maintain a lifestyle that made city life, and my professional life, more bearable. This might sound ridiculous to you, but it was very real to me.

In Bucerias, I only needed a few hundred dollars a month to live. I felt truly free for the first time in my life. Free to dance, to write, to wander, to dream, free to watch the sun set over the Pacific. It's amazing how little your practical self needs when you give your soul what it longs for.

These days I'm based up in Canada again, for as long as it feels right and makes sense. I'm still living by my new rules, though, and it's my inner artist who calls the shots. As long as her writing, dancing, and dreams take first priority, she's happy. And as long as she's happy, I'm happy. That works for me.

THE ARTIST'S WAY

Obviously, I don't know what your situation is. You might be completely out of touch with your artistic tendencies or you might be a fully actualized artist. Regardless, I hope there's something in this chapter that speaks to you and frees you to fly to the next level.

I grew up as the family "brain," the oldest child in a traditional nuclear family. My father is an engineer and my mother was a stay-at-home mom. I learned that life was about being practical; you make logical choices that increase your likelihood of traditional success. I fulfilled all of our culture's classic expectations for a "good" child: straight A's, university scholarships, becoming a doctor. Check, check, check.

Meanwhile, my younger sisters got to have all the fun. Tania, the next sister in line, began painting and drawing as soon as she could hold a crayon. Today, she's a missionary who uses her art to serve others. In her entire life, she's never worked at a job that didn't fulfill one of her two passions. It hasn't been easy, but she's never compromised who she is at her core.

My next sister, Vanessa, isn't creative in the traditional sense. Yet from a very young age she demonstrated two distinctive gifts: a fearless ability to communicate with and train animals and a determinedly creative approach to removing any obstacles that stood between her and her goals.

Vanessa officially declared her passion for horses when she was only six years old. Most little girls dream of having a horse and lump it in with other fairy tale dreams, such as living in a castle and marrying a prince. Little Vanessa, oblivious to "reality," was set on getting what she wanted. When she was seven, my parents paid for a set of riding lessons, thinking she'd get bored. She didn't.

When she was nine, my parents leased a horse for her to ride for one hour each week, thinking that she'd quickly tire of taking the bus to the stable. She didn't. She continued to beg for her own horse, and when she was eleven my father offered her a deal: he'd buy her a horse, if she found a way to pay for its food and board at the stable.

Thrilled by the challenge and her dream of a horse of her own, Vanessa got a paper route and cheerfully slugged her papers up the long and sometimes dizzyingly steep driveways of our mountain-side neighborhood. Later, when she was thirteen, she searched until she found a McDonald's that was willing to hire her (the minimum age for employment was actually fifteen). For years, she steadily paid her horse's rent, and quickly gained a reputation in the stable for her ability to calm difficult horses.

Talk about being dedicated to a dream! When we repeatedly demonstrate how passionate we are about something, through the efforts, sacrifices, and time we invest, the day will come when we finally get our full reward. In her early twenties, Vanessa decided to move by herself to Calgary, a real "cow town" where people walk the streets wearing Stetsons, and live and breathe horses. There, word of her creative ability to train and ride problem horses spread quickly.

The riding community embraced her, and one day a new friend gave her Leroy as a gift. Leroy was a problem horse that no one could seem to control—and also happened to be worth $50,000. Her friend also told Vanessa that she could board Leroy at the luxurious stables at her sprawling ranch, for just $100 a month, full room and board. That was less than Vanessa had paid to board her horse in Vancouver when she was thirteen years old.

I've got one more sister, and one more story. Growing up, I was strangely obsessed with pianos. My favorite friends were those who had pianos; when I went over to their houses after school, I would spend most of the afternoon sitting on their piano bench. I taught myself to play following the instructions in their piano books and begged my parents for years to buy me a piano. They finally did, when I was twelve.

I only took lessons for a couple of years, and then got bored with it and quit. My parents were baffled by my behavior until the divinely ordained reason for our having a piano, and for my piano obsession, announced itself. One day, when she was just three years old, my baby sister Laila clambered up onto my piano bench and began to play.

Growing up, Laila won all kinds of awards for classical piano, and even played the musical lead in her high school production of *Little Shop of Horrors*. But when she neared seventeen, the grown-ups around her agreed that it was time to stop "playing" and get practical. Laila applied for, and won, a full four-year scholarship to study Sciences at two top universities. Everything was moving along normally until, just months before her first class, she announced that she was moving across the country, alone, to enroll in a Fine Arts college. You can imagine the reaction at home.

At a remarkably young age, Laila knew that no matter how hard the road might turn out to be, she simply couldn't bring herself to deny her artistic side. She knew that music was the love of her life, and she wasn't willing to push it over to the side for any traditional measure of success.

In jazz circles, Laila has become one of the most highly acclaimed and respected artists of her generation. By her mid-twenties, she was regularly invited to teach jazz workshops at Stanford, had played both Carnegie Hall and the Kennedy Center, and had won national jazz awards for both composer of the year and keyboardist of the year. She's toured the globe with Grammy award–winning artists, and I personally witnessed legendary jazz diva Diana Krall shouting compliments from the first row while Laila played and sang on stage.

One Christmas, Laila kick-started my own artistic recovery by giving me the Julia Cameron book that I mentioned earlier: *The Artist's Way: A Spiritual Path to Higher Creativity*. Cameron's book helped me reconnect with and haul out the latent artist I had hidden so deeply inside, and quieted the disdainful critic in my head that had, and still does have, so much to say.

I learned how to play again, and I discovered that once you begin the journey of artistic re-discovery, anything is possible. Cameron taught me that living an artistic life doesn't have to mean being poor, and that divine intervention kicks in as soon as you take your first step towards any dream that delights your inner artist.

Though our spiritual perspectives differ somewhat, Cameron has been one of the most powerful, liberating influences on the shape of my life, and taught me to expect the inevitable miracles that accompany our creative efforts.

"When we open ourselves to our creativity, we open ourselves to the creator's creativity within us and our lives," she writes. Sure enough, whenever I took a dance class, writing class, or photography class, these artistic baby steps brought about all kinds of changes in the architecture and fate of my entire life, extending far beyond simple moments spent dancing or writing.

I began my literary career writing fiction and travel stories. The first article that I ever submitted and published was about the culinary delights of a cycling trip through Tuscany. They featured it, in color, on the front page of the Saturday travel section of a major regional newspaper. They paid me with a remarkably hideous sweatshirt, but no paycheck could have been sweeter than that first moment when I saw my byline in print.

When I first started, I never imagined that I would become a professional freelance writer and a published author. I submitted my travel story to that newspaper because, while on a trip with him, my previously mentioned artistic then-boyfriend had mocked my writing dreams and had told me that nothing that I ever wrote would get published. That travel article was my first freelance writing piece; my nationally published articles now number in the hundreds.

When you open yourself to creativity and the hand of the "great creator," there's no limit to the ways in which seemingly inconsequential steps will turn your whole life into a kaleidoscope of "coincidences" and color.

THE ULTIMATE TREASURE HUNT: FINDING YOUR INNER ARTIST

Who do you envy? Does it bug you that your brother sings in a "stupid" band? Do you make fun of how bad they are, while secretly wishing that you could rip the mike out of his hands and be up there in his place?

Does it annoy you when your friend traipses off to Provence for those art courses, especially given how amateurish her watercolors are? Who does she think she is, calling herself an *artist*? You don't even know how to paint, but inside you tell yourself that if you ever won a million dollars, and had the time and money to run around the world taking fancy classes, you'd be far better than she is.

I once met a photographer who married a successful stockbroker. Her husband made so much money that he could happily sponsor her photography career, without making a dent in their lifestyle. I felt sad after spending time with them. It just didn't seem fair!

I learned from Cameron that envy and jealousy are giant red flags that show you where your inner artist is feeling ripped off. Whenever you notice this, I recommend that you take some kind of immediate action, however small. You might not be able to go to Provence right now (or perhaps you could), but you can surely go out and buy some paints or sign up for a community watercolor class. You might not be able to replace your brother in his band, but who knows: he might just let you sing back-up, if you'd only ask.

When I recognized my red flag of envy, I knew that I had to indulge my inner photographer. I bought myself a "real" camera and signed up for a basic photography course. I wandered around, taking as many pictures as I wanted to. I submitted photos to magazines, and to a couple of gallery competitions. I soon got to see my photos in print (including one national magazine cover photo) and even enjoyed having a couple of modest gallery shows.

For a couple of years, my inner photographer got a lot of my attention, until I felt that that chapter of my creative life had been completed. Today, when I meet a full-time photographer, the jealousy is gone. Instead, I'm free to feel appreciation for their work.

I still find it hard to watch professional shows by more accomplished dance colleagues or world-class flamenco artists. That red flag tells me that I can't let up on my dance dream just yet, as I obviously still have much of the journey left to go.

Ask yourself these questions: What aspects of your life are trying to get your attention? Are there certain people you feel jealous of? Are there things you'd love to try but always dismiss as being silly? Are there things that you know you'd do, if it weren't for the fact that you're too old or that you don't have enough money? There, my friend, is where you'll find your treasure.

PLAY: THE FAST LANE TO CREATIVITY

If you can't think of any artistic people that you envy, and don't think you have creative leanings, I encourage you to simply start to play. Get out of your head, and get into the rich world around you. Think of the things you loved to do when you were little—could you start doing any of them again, now?

When was the last time that you went to a play or built a sand castle? Wander through a used bookstore and instead of buying something in your usual comfort zone, buy piles of books on fascinating quirky subjects that interest you. If money's tight, spend an afternoon at the local library. Reconnect with color, music, stories, and adventure. Get out the catalog for your local community center and sign up for a course that sounds fun.

Interrupt your usual routine. Start going for long aimless walks and listen to what starts to burble up inside your mind. Write pages in a journal about nothing in particular. For me, traveling always works—I always seem to find myself, and aspects of myself that I didn't know existed, whenever I go somewhere new.

When you give yourself permission to play, your whole world expands and becomes sweeter. You'll find that you laugh more, finally take those longed-for risks, and develop an appetite for adventure and new experiences. Friends, family, and work colleagues might start to comment that you're a lot more fun to be around. You'll make new, fun, adventurous friends through your new activities. It's contagious, too—you'll be surprised at how many people in your life will rise up to join you. Best of all, you'll eventually discover that you like yourself, and your life, a whole lot more.

I also guarantee that your whole body will rejoice in all this new fun. You'll have more energy and enjoy better health and happier, more playful moods.

As Cameron taught me, I'd like you to once and for all erase the following phrases from your vocabulary: "It's too late," "I'm too old," "I'd feel silly," "I wouldn't be any good at it," "It's just not practical." Got it? Now go out and have some fun.

11

FIND YOUR PERFECT BALANCE

I'D PROPPED ONE leg up against the tiled shower wall and was drying myself off with my favorite fluffy towel when I first noticed it. I passed the towel over my left foot again in disbelief and then grabbed my big toe with my hand. I ran my finger down the inside of my foot and was shocked to find that along the top third of my foot I couldn't feel anything other than an uncomfortable pressure, as if my foot were asleep.

Over the next few weeks, the numbness continued to progress, and one day, as I was giving myself a pedicure, I noticed that my right toe was also starting to go numb in the same area. Now I was scared. I'd had frequent headaches for a couple of months, but I'd written them off as migraines due to the stress of planning my upcoming wedding. I'd also noticed that sometimes when I was writing emails I'd think of a specific word, yet another completely unrelated word would come out through my fingers onto the screen.

We doctors notoriously prefer to diagnose and treat ourselves (not recommended, by the way), but once the wedding was over and life was back to normal, I finally summoned up the courage to see a neurologist. With a pained look on his face he told me what I'd feared. Though he tried to reassure me several times that it was unlikely to be something serious, he knew that I knew too much. When it comes to our symptoms and our bodies, doctors get no bliss from ignorance.

"If you do have multiple sclerosis," he told me, "it's the mildest case I've ever seen." Neither of us mentioned the word "tumor," though we both knew that was also a possibility.

My first reactions were grief, self-pity, and anger. How could this happen, and why now? I'd just gotten married to the man of my dreams, my career as a speaker and media expert was taking off internationally, and in the previous month I'd had more prestigious flamenco gigs than ever before. In all my life, I'd never been so excited about life.

Then, the next day, I suddenly got it.

I'd been so distracted by my symptoms and all the exciting events in my life that I'd forgotten my own principles. Despite what I constantly teach other people about body language, I'd been so overwhelmed by this unexpected situation that I never stopped to ask my body what it was trying to tell me.

The instant I stopped and listened, the word came to me swiftly and clearly.

Balance.

I almost cried with relief. My body was telling me, through these symptoms, and possibly through a serious illness, that I needed to slow down. As much as I wanted to do everything, and as much as I was trying to do everything, I couldn't keep going at that pace and expect to maintain my health. I also knew, in that moment, that the key to my healing, no matter what my diagnosis turned out to be, would be bringing my life back into balance, in all aspects, as quickly as possible.

A SILENT EPIDEMIC

Last year, the largest chapter, worldwide, of the International Federation of University Women chose me from a list of some of the most impressive speakers in the nation. As their twenty-fifth annual lecturer, I joined the ranks of an intimidating list of past speakers, including one of the most famous journalists in the history of Canadian television, a renowned female astronaut, and the Chief Justice of the Federal Supreme Court.

At first I thought it must have been a mistake, until the event planner told me why this group of brilliant, hyper-educated women had picked me.

"We desperately need balance," she told me, "and we thought you would be the perfect person to teach us how to find it."

I constantly hear complaints and concerns about life balance from meeting planners, human resource managers, coaching clients, and most people around me. It seems that creating a healthy and meaningful balance in our day-to-day lives is the most common personal challenge for people in our society today. And it's my biggest challenge, too.

Check out this list of quotes that I've collected from clients and seminar participants:

"I don't have any time for myself in my schedule."

"I have too much to do to fit into too little time, and I feel overwhelmed all the time."

"I need more fun and freedom in my life."

"Balance—that's the hardest thing for me. Everything that I want to do feels like a priority, and I don't see how I can give anything up."

Sound familiar?

WAKE UP, BRUSH YOUR TEETH,
COMMIT TO BALANCE

You're not alone if you believe that a healthy, well-balanced life is only for more disciplined types, people who probably woke up one day (perhaps at birth), and decided that from that point on they would live in blissful, meaningful, and highly productive balance. If you have children, you probably think that "life balance" is a cruel joke invented by the childless. Perhaps, before reading my opening story in this chapter, you thought that life coaches and life balance experts like me must have mastered this balance thing years ago, and live our days in perfectly organized serenity. Ha! I wish.

Life is dynamic: Circumstances change, we change, the people around us change, and you constantly have to readjust to keep it all chugging along harmoniously. I've learned the hard way, and not just once, that balance isn't something you just create one day, and then can forget about.

To live in balance, we need to consciously commit to it every day. Just like you stick to a healthy eating plan or an exercise program, balance is something that you decide that you're going to create, every day, in order to reap its many benefits. It becomes part of your daily routine, like brushing your teeth.

You might not always feel like brushing your teeth or taking the time for breakfast, but you've likely learned over the years that these are habits worth doing, despite the time they take out of your day. I despise flossing, but I've learned that if I want to keep myself out of the dentist's chair, I've got to keep doing it, daily.

Your life may be so out of control and busy that you don't know where to start. Or perhaps you fear that you're so far gone, you'll never get yourself and your life back. As they say in the twelve-step programs, life is about "progress, not perfection." Any time you discover that you've fallen off the balance wagon, whether it's for a day or for the last few years, you can renew your commitment and start fresh, today.

BACK-TO-BALANCE BASICS

Achieving wellness and balance isn't rocket science. You really don't even need me to tell you what you need to do. You already know it, and my words are just a helpful reminder, a wake-up call. The most critical basics of balance are truly ridiculously simple:

Sleep well, eat well, and exercise well. That's it.

Of course, that's not the full extent of my advice for you, but it's where I'd like you to start.

In the face of my recent health scare, these were the first principles that I fell back on, the critical first steps that I took towards regaining my balance and well-being. When I get busy and stressed, I stay up late, skip meals, and put off exercise for "later." I end up tired, hungry, and frazzled, and without enough energy and concentration to effectively perform through a busy day.

Why is it that as soon as life gets crowded, we push sleep, good nutrition, and exercise out of the way, to make room for what we think is "more important"? We've got it backwards! We should see these good health basics as the foundation of our day, the non-negotiable framework of balance in our lives, rather than considering them as disposable options.

If you get enough sleep, eat healthy food throughout the day, and fit in a walk or a workout whenever you can, you'll dramatically increase your ability to cope with stress and will improve your capacity to perform under pressure. You'll be less likely to burn out, you'll enjoy better moods and be less irritable, and you'll also be much less likely to get sick.

The first step I took was to make sure I got to bed before midnight, every night (no more late-night web-surfing, TV, or email). This is one of my biggest hurdles, something that's almost impossible for me to do on my own. I remind myself of a perpetual two-year-old who refuses to go to bed early because she thinks she'll miss out on all the fun.

Research shows that you significantly improve your chances of success if you enlist the help of others to reach your goals. I asked Armando to help me with this one: If he catches me at my computer past 11 pm, he's authorized to drag me into the bedroom, no matter how much I might insist that I need "just five more minutes."

In my quest for better balance, I also focused on eating more fruits or vegetables with every meal and throughout the day. Despite what I know about the basics of good nutrition, it's not always easy to live what I preach. When things get crazy, I tend to skimp on protein and fill up with feel-good carbs, so I started eating more lean protein, like egg whites, fish, and chicken. These fundamental elements are so basic to a healthy life—yet here I am, the nutrition expert, having to remind myself to eat my veggies. So don't feel bad if you have to work at it, too!

We also recently added a dog to our family (a rescue from the Los Cabos Humane Society), and he has done wonders for our health and wellness. His crazy antics constantly make us laugh (boosting our immunity and helping us relieve stress), and he also obliges us to take him out for long walks in the fresh air, twice a day.

You don't need to join a gym or hire a personal trainer (or get a dog) in order to start getting more exercise. Ever since I was a teenager, going for walks has been my primary way of ensuring that I stay in shape and maintain my weight. Walking is easy on your joints and body, and is great for relieving stress. Best of all, it's free! Dancing is another great way to get exercise without even noticing that you're working out. Check out the classes offered by your local community center, or search online for classes in your area. Trust me—you're never too old and it's never too late to start dancing!

THE BIG LIE

If a genie appeared in front of you, right now, and offered to grant you three wishes, what would be your first wish?

If you're like me, and most other people, you'd probably say: "Give me a million dollars! No, wait! Make it *ten* million dollars!"

If money isn't the first thing that comes to your mind, I'm impressed, but chances are still pretty good that it would be somewhere in there, among your "big three." In our culture, we've been sold the idea that money equals happiness. If we're not feeling happy or fulfilled, we just need to earn more, buy more, and have more, to feel better.

We live in the future, dreaming of the day we'll finally have that income, or that home, or that luxurious trip—won't life feel so good then? We get there, and it feels great for a little while, but then one day we realize that we're still our normal selves, problems and all. We feel ripped off. Next, without stopping to consider that our greatest fulfillment might lie elsewhere, we focus on getting still *more* money and stuff, hoping that the "next level up" will feel better.

If you're living in poverty, or are saddled by huge debt, studies have shown that you *will* probably be happier once you have more money and can comfortably afford life's basic necessities. However, once you have more money and things than you actually need, you're statistically less likely to be happy than that "less successful" person next to you, who has just enough to enjoy a comfortable life.

A woman came up to me once after I talked about this in a seminar. "You're absolutely right," she told me. "I work in one of the world's most exclusive resorts and you wouldn't believe the number of guests who fly in on their private planes, rent our best villas, and are totally miserable."

I'm not saying you should dedicate yourself to making sure that you never have more than the basic necessities in life, nor am I saying that if you're financially successful you're destined to be miserable. I do encourage you to remember that money alone isn't likely to bring lasting satisfaction, and that you'd be wise to simultaneously give attention to the elements that we know create real happiness and fulfillment.

PEOPLE FIRST, LIFE LATER

I have a major deadline for tomorrow night, and as I write this I'm not sure how I'm going to get it all done. This morning, I got an email from my friend Catherine, asking if we're still on for lunch tomorrow. The last time we tried to get together, five months ago, she canceled because of an important meeting. We scheduled tomorrow's lunch over a month ago, but I only got word of this deadline yesterday. When I told Catherine, she said, "You're nutty to try to meet me in the middle of all this, are you sure you don't want to cancel?"

Here's what I emailed back: "I teach people that they have to seize the moment and carve out time for friends and the people that matter. If we don't, life rushes by and always gives us some 'urgent' reason to put work before people. Years pass, as we keep saying 'We should really have lunch soon.' So, we're going to have lunch, tomorrow."

Years from now, I probably won't remember the deadline, but I might not forget that I canceled my lunch with Catherine. She could end up moving and I'd never see her again. I've lost count of the number of times that this happened to me in Cabo's large ex-pat community. In fact, I just got an email yesterday from someone whom I tried repeatedly to have lunch with over the past two years, but was always too busy. To be fair, she did invite me a couple times after we met, during a busy time of my life when I "had to" say no. Later, it was her turn to be "too busy," as she got her new business off the ground.

"I'm finally free!" she wrote, "How about we finally have that lunch?" I still haven't written her back because I'm not sure how to tell her that I've moved back to Canada. We could have been great friends, and we both knew it when we first met. We just never found the time to make that happen. We assumed that life would wait for us.

To guarantee yourself the best chance at a healthy, happy life, make room in your life for people. We've already discussed how important it is to look after yourself, so you know that I'm not suggesting that you neglect your own self-care to meet the needs of others. But, in these busy times, it's important that we really understand how essential it is to make people a priority. In study after study, positive contact with other people is shown to be the best predictor of good health and happiness.

By nature I'm a workaholic, and have gotten worse since I've found my true life's work. I happily work round the clock, barely looking up from my computer. When Armando first complained that he felt jealous of my laptop, I was mildly annoyed.

Shortly after, I realized that I needed a serious attitude makeover. My computer, or my website, will never be able to hug me at the end of a long day. They can't hold my hand, or walk on the beach with me, or accompany me through a long, leisurely dinner. I might feel annoyed or stressed out by the people in my life who make "demands" when I'm on a tight deadline. But I know that if those people were to give up on me and disappear, my life, projects and all, would be devastatingly empty.

As many successful, hard-driving people have discovered, "it's lonely at the top." Career successes and life triumphs lose their sweetness very quickly if there aren't beloved people around to celebrate them with you.

MAKE YOUR DREAMS A PRIORITY

How did you feel after reading the chapter about life dreams? Perhaps you're allowing yourself, for the first time in years, to consider ideas, projects, and passions that you'd forgotten or given up on. You might be feeling a tingle of excitement, or hope—the dreams in your heart really could become reality!

But first, to give your dreams their very best chance, there's something that I should warn you about. If it hasn't happened already, your life may soon divide in two. In one hand, you'll have your everyday life, rushing along, full of demands, commitments, and "necessary" activities. In the other hand, you'll have your fragile, precious dream or goal.

Everyday life tends to have immediate, short-term deadlines. Your dreams, by nature, don't. We think of our dreams as something we'll do "someday"—maybe we'll take the first step next week, or next month, after we get through this busy time. Yet life rarely stops to wait for dreams, and before we know it, years have passed and we haven't moved more than a step or two closer to our dream. Or perhaps we haven't done anything at all.

Our dreams wait patiently, reminding us of their presence through tugs in the heart and waves of regret when we see someone else doing what we dream of. But the voice of your dream usually isn't as loud and insistent as the demands of daily life. You might encounter the neglected voice of your dreams through depression, or frustration, or even physical symptoms, without realizing what's really going on.

Your dreams deserve as important a place in your life as sleep, good nutrition, exercise, and time with loved ones. Just like the other things in life that count most, you need to commit to incorporating elements of your dream into your life on a daily basis, or they simply will never happen. At the end of life, nobody wants to realize that they're leaving without having experienced the one thing they dreamed of most. Yet it's so easy to let everything else eat up our attention, and our days.

Now when I decide whether to say yes or no to a new opportunity, I consider it in the context of my dreams and important (but often non-urgent) priorities. For example, I cleared my schedule for this month in order to focus on finishing this book. Publishing a book is something I've wanted to do since I was a little girl. I've received a ton of phone calls and emails all month long, and invitations to attend social events or to appear on a radio show or in a magazine. I agreed to a few of the biggest interviews, because they also fit my dream: Media exposure is essential to getting my name out there, which will ultimately result in more people reading my book.

I simply said no to almost everything else. However, there was one particularly tough choice. A producer called me and offered me the opportunity to be a major contributor to a wellness television show, which airs internationally and films during this month— my "finish my book" month.

So how did I make my decision? First, I considered the fact that the show focused on weight loss. Though I have a degree in nutrition and do speak and write about how to lose and manage your weight, educating people about that isn't a primary part of my dream and mission in this life. Also, I would have had to film in several cities, which would have made finishing my book extremely stressful. To be able to do it all, I'd probably have had to sacrifice part of my recent holidays spent with Armando and his family in the mountains of Mexico. That trip was particularly special, as we hadn't spent the holidays with his family in four years.

I followed my own balance formula and considered this difficult decision in the light of my priorities: my health (the need to minimize stress and chaos); my most important people (Armando and his family); my life dreams (my book is more important than a TV show); and my mission (though working with the media is part of my mission, the show topic isn't one that I'm truly passionate about). Looking at it this way, that "agonizing" choice became surprisingly clear and simple. On top of that, I knew from experience that when you give up something in the name of balance, love, and true priorities, the opportunity almost always gets presented again, and in an even more perfect form. I've found that, as a rule, life rewards us when we make difficult but principled choices.

I've given you a lot of information in this chapter, so I thought it might be helpful to summarize some of my top life-balance tips. Whether you implement all of them at once or just one at a time, you'll find that each makes a significant difference in the quality of your life and health:

> *Get more than seven hours of sleep a night*

This will boost your immune system, improve your mood, help you handle stress better, and make you more likely to achieve and maintain a healthy weight. Did you know that if you sleep less than seven hours a night, you're significantly more likely to be overweight? When you don't get enough sleep, your body secretes hormones that actually make you eat more. Do you need any more motivation than that?

❧ *Start your day with a balanced breakfast, and eat healthy foods throughout the day*

Eating breakfast will give you more energy, help you concentrate better, and protect you from weight gain. Eating healthy foods regularly throughout the day will maintain your energy level and boost your mood and vitality. You'll feel great!

❧ *Get moving, and walk whenever you can*

Look for opportunities to move: take the stairs, go out dancing, park a few blocks farther away, go for a walk in the park on your lunch break. Get in the habit of taking a walk with your spouse or partner, or a friend, every evening—it'll benefit both your relationship and your health.

❧ *Keep your values and dreams in mind every time you decide whether or not to take on a new commitment*

What matters most to you in life? Your health? Your family and friends? Your dream of opening your own business? Whenever someone asks you to commit to something new (even if it's just for one day or one hour), ask yourself if it fits with your most important values and goals, or if it will take time away from them.

❧ *Put a priority on the activities that boost your health and happiness*

Activities that increase your health and happiness will help you be more effective and productive in every aspect of your life. Spend time with people who make you laugh and leave you feeling energized; make time for hobbies that relieve stress and fill you with passion and joy; carve out and protect the essential "me time" that lets you de-stress and unwind.

❧ *Remember to have fun along the way*

Life is too potentially wonderful to be too serious about everything. Remember that "everything happens for a reason," and resolve to make lemonade out of any lemons that life hands you. Take time to laugh and play and enjoy the wonderful people, places, and events that you come across in your journey.

Of course, even if you follow the balance principles that we've talked about, you are still going to have days or times that race by, seemingly beyond your control. Keep these fundamentals of balance, health, and happiness in mind, and you'll have the tools to reorient and refresh your life whenever you need to.

As for my potential diagnosis of MS, I had an MRI of both my neck and spine a few months later and they were totally clear. As I write this, my symptoms are almost completely back to normal.

Come what may, I'm so grateful to have these principles of balance and basic wellness to fall back on whenever I need them. As is so often the case with life's curveballs, my scary neurological symptoms turned out to be a blessing. Today, I enjoy a far better and far healthier life as a result of my scare. Thanks to my body and this experience, I've renewed my own commitment to balance—and I hope this chapter has both inspired you and helped you to renew yours.

6

MAKE ROOM FOR
THE DIVINE

12

BLESS YOUR HEALTH
AND SELF THROUGH SPIRITUAL
PRACTICE

One day, after I'd finished giving a keynote lecture to a group of physicians, a slightly built, dark-skinned doctor made his way down the lecture hall staircase. He waited patiently beside the podium as a long line of his colleagues introduced themselves to me and asked me questions.

When they had left, he came over and stood before me.

"Do you believe in God?" he asked me, his words made musical by his accent.

Somewhat taken aback, I paused, and then responded: "Yes, I do."

"Then why didn't you mention that anywhere in your talk?" he asked. "Don't you think that's just as important, or more important, than anything else you just said?"

Rather than feeling offended, I happened to agree with him. In fact, I told him this: "It's quite strange that you would come up to me and say this right now. When I was driving here this morning, I said my usual prayer that the event would be a success and that the people would leave feeling hopeful and inspired. At that moment, I realized that though I rely on my faith to get through so many aspects of life, I almost never mention that in my speeches. I give people all kinds of tips about life, but often don't share my biggest tip of all.

"I asked for guidance about whether I needed to start talking more about this in my work. And here you are—with the answer."

He smiled, inclined his head towards me, turned, and walked out the door.

Just as I'm never quite sure how to incorporate God into my speeches, it's been just as challenging for me to decide how to incorporate God into this book. There are plenty of famous sages out there who write entire books about God, but it's not really what most people would expect from a doctor. I suspect that many aspects of this book aren't what most people would expect from a doctor, but I write about the things I do because I want to help you create a better life on many different levels.

If I'm going to serve you completely, and if I'm going to claim to teach you everything I know about creating a happier, healthier life, I've got to talk about spirituality and the divine. If the word "God" makes you uncomfortable, substitute whatever word or term feels right for you (e.g., "universe," "higher power," "creator," etc.).

When things were darkest in my life, I didn't really have any form of regular spiritual practice. I attended church with my family growing up but didn't pay much attention, and I didn't really think about spiritual issues at all during my university and medical training. I don't remember a single course in my medical school that talked about religion or spirituality, except in psychiatry when they taught us that some delusions were considered acceptable if they were shared by a large group of people in a religious context(!).

I recently came across a research review paper titled "Religious Commitment and Health Status," in the *Archives of Family*

Medicine, that reported: 1) 95 percent of Americans believe in God; 2) more than 50 percent of people pray daily; and 3) almost 50 percent of patients want their physician to pray with them. I am ashamed to say that in almost ten years of medical practice, I've never prayed with a patient. I have prayed frequently and fervently for patients in particularly desperate situations, but I've limited it to the privacy of my own personal office.

It amazes me that I was and still am so self-conscious about talking about spiritual issues with patients, despite what I know about the huge impact that spiritual and religious practices have on people's overall health and life. I can't make it up to all those patients that I never told, but I can try to compensate now, by sharing what I know with you.

YOUR PERSONAL PRACTICE

What kinds of spiritual or religious practices do you participate in or enjoy? Are they a regular part of your life?

I recently read another article called "The Psychological and Physical Benefits of Spiritual/Religious Practices" by sociologist Dr. Ellen Idler, published in UCLA's *Spirituality in Higher Education* newsletter. In it, Idler describes some of the surprisingly versatile ways that different people undertake spiritual and religious practices. Her list of examples includes: meditating, singing with a choir, going on a weekend retreat, taking the sacraments, listening to inspired speakers like Dr. Martin Luther King Jr., dancing at a wedding, lighting Hanukkah candles, saying prayers, and contemplating a sunset view.

I'll ask you a different way, from the broader and more creative perspective just described: What brings you closer to God? What practices or activities resonate with or inspire you? What could you start doing today that would bring you more in touch with this element of life?

Have you had the experience of doing something wonderful, particularly something that connected you to the essence of life, love, humanity, and faith, something so fulfilling that you immediately said to yourself, "I really need to do this more often"? What was it? When was it? Did you do it more often? If not, why not? What's stopping you?

We humans are such a funny sort. We know what's good for us, we know what we love, we know what inspires and moves and elevates us, but sometimes it's just so hard to do it. The things that seem easiest to do are the everyday, the mundane, the "to-do" lists, the uninspiring tasks. It's such a strange phenomenon, but it's how most of us are. My goal in this chapter is to provide you with some surprising information about the connections between spiritual practice and health, to motivate you to make more room for this blessed part of life in your life.

You'll notice that I refer to both "religion" and "spirituality." Though I myself am a practicing Christian, I know that many people react negatively to the word "religion." When I write about religion here, I'm using a definition similar to that put forward by the authors of the above-mentioned review paper from the *Archives of Family Medicine*: "Religious commitment refers to the participation in or endorsement of practices, beliefs, attitudes, or sentiments that are associated with an organized community of faith."

Most of the research done in the area of spirituality and health examines elements of organized religious practices, as these are far easier to quantify and study than more vague "spiritual" activities. However, though I'm going to emphasize religion-related studies, it doesn't mean that I'm negating the power of simple, unorganized spiritual practices to bless your life and health.

THE KEY TO A HAPPIER, HEALTHIER, LONGER LIFE

When people get sick, they often feel like they've lost control of their lives and the ultimate outcome. On the contrary, a growing body of research shows that we—and a power "higher" than us—have a lot more potential to impact that outcome, and our overall well-being, than most of us realize.

How would you like to dramatically increase your chances of living longer? A classic study that looked at almost 100,000 people found that those who went to church weekly enjoyed 50 percent fewer deaths from heart disease. Another study, which followed over 5,000 people for twenty-eight years also found that weekly church attendance significantly improved long-term survival.

It's well-documented that people who regularly attend religious services generally smoke less, drink less, and have less casual sex, all of which naturally protect their health. But, before you assume that it's simply "clean living" that explains the increased longevity and health, consider the following study, published in the *Journal of Religion and Health*.

A group of researchers explored the relationship between religiosity and high blood pressure by comparing the blood pressures of smokers who rated religion as important to smokers for whom religious beliefs were unimportant. The smokers who considered religion an important part of their lives were more than seven times less likely to have an abnormally high blood pressure reading.

According to a report published in the *British Journal of Psychiatry*, close to half the population of the Western World can expect one or more episodes of depression in their lifetime. If you'd prefer to be part of the Western population's "happy half," spiritual and religious practices will significantly increase your odds of enjoying a depression-free life.

One study, done on almost two thousand twins, found that those who were more religious had a significantly lower risk of current or lifetime depression. Another study, which examined religious beliefs and experiences ("intrinsic religiosity") in a group of elderly ill patients, found that patients with strong intrinsic religious beliefs recovered significantly more quickly from episodes of mild to moderate depression. Another review that looked at over ten years of psychiatric research studies found that 84 percent of all studies reported a positive effect of religious commitment on mental health. That's powerful stuff!

In the article I mentioned earlier, Idler explores the multi-faceted reasons for the impressive effect of religious behavior on mental and physical health. People who associate with a religious or spiritual group enjoy tightly knit social circles, which naturally provide many different kinds of support and help them deal with stress.

Idler also points out that churches typically provide a welcoming and nurturing environment for people across all age groups and social classes. Usually, when you walk into a church or spiritual meeting, people will embrace you with smiles and a warm handshake, and will be thrilled to see you return. Given today's climate of social isolation and obsession with electronic communication, this kind of unconditional human contact and interaction is needed more now than perhaps any other time in human history.

Also, more than ever, we all need to rest. Most religious or spiritual practices are both relaxing and health-promoting in nature. Sitting quietly in mass, taking in the magnificence of a spring garden, or listening to a beautiful choir may be the only time you really stop and sit still in your entire busy week. Taking a few minutes to sit in silence in the morning, to pray and meditate on the things that are most important to you, can be an anchor of peace and stillness that grounds your entire day.

POWERFUL PRAYERS

Years ago, when I first began exploring the world outside traditional medicine, a wise mentor pointed me towards the work of a fellow medical doctor, Larry Dossey. I am especially passionate about, and often refer to, his landmark book, *The Power of Prayer and the Practice of Medicine.*

In this book, Dossey explores the realities of the relationship between prayer, our health, and "miracle cures," and reveals many surprising facts that remain seared in my brain to this day. The biggest single message that I took away is this: Often, the most powerful prayer you can ask is one that doesn't ask for any specific outcome. To quote Dossey, "some studies, in fact, showed that a simple 'Thy will be done' approach was quantitatively more powerful than when specific results were held in the mind."

The twelve-step recovery programs (which deliberately aren't associated with any particular religion or spiritual group) have a similar approach, reflected in Step 11: "We sought to improve our conscious contact with God as we understood Him, praying only for knowledge of His will for us and the power to carry that out." I think they're right—in many of my own life situations, I have found that the most effective solution is to simply ask for help and then hand over the reins.

THE PERFECTION IN PAIN

Dossey also writes that despite our most fervent prayers, life events and illnesses don't always turn out as we might hope. Or at least that's the way it looks, from our small, human perspective. We may find ourselves burdened by a terrifying disease and pray desperately to be cured, and then feel abandoned when that doesn't happen.

In our limited human understanding of what's "best" for us, we naturally assume that the best outcome always equals healing or avoidance of pain and suffering. As I've mentioned earlier, I think our lives might turn out disastrously if we were truly able to independently create whatever we wanted. We'd also lose so many valuable lessons if things always turned out "perfectly."

Of course, it depends on your definition of perfection. I've decided that perfection is simply whatever is best for my life and development right now—no matter how unappealing it may seem to me in the moment. It's all good, and it's all for my good. I've found that having this attitude when tough times arrive makes such a difference to the entire experience. Though believe me, I still get shaken up when those tough times first show up.

One of my major lessons in this area came to me through a series of events in my mom's life. When I was seventeen, she was diagnosed with an aggressive kind of breast cancer. As soon as she got the news, they booked her for major surgery, but the first available date was several weeks away.

I'll never forget the day she took me aside in the kitchen after school and told me about her diagnosis. In the same breath, she also told me that in the weeks before her surgery she and my father were going alone together to Hawaii, and that I'd have to stay at home and look after my three younger sisters.

Their time in Hawaii was the first time in almost two decades that my mother had an extended time period without us kids, and it provided a rare chance to reflect upon her life and its meaning.

"It suddenly hit me that I might not have much time left to live," she told me later, "and I realized that my life until that point had been more about duty than it had been about truly living."

It was true—she had been a fantastic mom to all of us, and a wonderful wife and homemaker, but she worked and tended us from morning until night and didn't really have any of her own pursuits or personal space.

After my mom recovered from her surgery, she began making up for lost time. She called up long-lost friends, became the hospitality director at her church, and focused on loving our family and herself more than on making sure all the necessary household tasks got done.

Before her cancer, we weren't a very close family, and conflict often ruled the day. After her cancer, our family fell in love with itself. To this day, almost twenty years later, my parents still act like love-struck teenagers. I've also received approximately ten times as many hugs in the last twenty years than I did in the first seventeen.

We all bloomed because of my mom's brush with mortality. Though of course she's very fortunate to have survived, she would never have volunteered to go through the fear and series of surgeries she was forced to endure. Nonetheless, my mom's battle with cancer was one of the biggest blessings that ever happened to our family.

DANCING WITH THE DIVINE

Make room for the divine in your life. Don't wait until things get difficult to reach for those spiritual beliefs and practices that so enrich your life. Live each day in a spiritual context. In the big picture, as a higher power might see it, what matters most? Are you doing it? Are you living it?

Throughout this book I've discussed a variety of steps you can take to improve the quality of your life and health. If you connect with and honor your most authentic self; treat yourself with love;

listen to and take good care of your body; nurture and create healthy relationships; balance your life; and dare to dream, you're virtually guaranteed to have a dramatically better experience of life here on earth.

You can magnify the benefits of each concept exponentially by making ever more room for the divine. If you make spiritual principles, guidance and practice the foundation for it all, you'll discover the experience of true meaning in your life, in every dimension of your existence.

In the words of Rick Warren, author of *The Purpose-Driven Life*: "When life has meaning, you can bear almost anything; without it, nothing is bearable."

7

MAKE "SOMEDAY" TODAY

13

STOP WAITING FOR TOMORROW—
MAKE "SOMEDAY" TODAY!

HERE WE ARE. Are you feeling excited about your life? What changes have you made already, as a result of the chapters that you've already read?

First of all, before I continue, I'd like to let you know that I'd love to hear your story. I'm passionate about this book and the other projects that I'm involved in because I want to make a real, lasting difference to your life.

If my words have helped you in any significant way, or have helped bring about miraculous changes in your life, please tell me about it. You can contact me through my website, www.susanbiali.com. Who knows—if you'd like to share your dreams or inspiring story with the world, you might even end up in my next book! More important though, I'd love to know that I've contributed to the quality of your life journey. That's what this is all about.

DON'T WAIT FOR "SOMEDAY"

Are you a self-help junkie? I used to be. I know lots of people who read the books, listen to the CDs, and go to as many seminars and retreats as they can. You might (and probably do) experience a "high" in the moment—it feels so good to read that book, or to listen to that speaker, or to share with that group. But when it's all over, you're back in your life, back to the same old same old. What do you do to fix it? Sign up for the next feel-good seminar!

I don't have a problem with the concept of self-help—it has helped me immensely, and I'm a huge advocate of lifelong learning. I just worry that all that "learning" might give you the illusion that you're actually taking action in your life. It's true that learning itself is an action, but you also need to act on what you learn.

What's your vision for your life after having read this book? How are you going to live differently from this day forward?

If you haven't downloaded the free workbook from my website yet, do that now (at www.susanbiali.com/workbook.html). The questions and exercises in the workbook will help you review and record the changes that you'd like to make. You'll then have dated lists to refer to that will keep you accountable to yourself.

Whenever I start to feel blue or lost in my life, I get out my own lists. Some are in notebooks that I've handled so often the pages are starting to fall out. Not only does it feel great to see that I've actually accomplished a lot of what I'd written, it also shows me where my self and life still need work. It can also remind me of promises that I once made to myself that I might need to resurrect.

What are you putting off, right now, for "someday"? Do you have a dream, but the financial timing isn't quite right? Get started anyway. Take whatever first small step you can. I've said it before: You'll be amazed at the things that will happen as a result of simply taking a small step towards your dreams. The timing will never be perfect. So many people waste so much time waiting for a moment that will never arrive. Life doesn't wait for us.

If your dream is a trip to Italy, you might legitimately not be able to afford to go—right now. I'm not suggesting you go into debt to live that dream. However, you can take small steps that bring you closer to it, or even let you start enjoying the experience now, without even getting on a plane.

If money's the problem, you can still make a realistic plan for when you'd like to go, and collect and browse through travel brochures. Sign up for a reward miles program and start earning points towards a free airline ticket. Go to your local library and rent a documentary about Italy or a feature film that takes place there. Go to your gourmet grocer, or to "Little Italy," if your town has one. Buy some specialty foods, get a bottle of cheap but delicious Italian wine, and whip up an Italian meal with real Italian ingredients. Have a "Pre-Italy Party" at home, topped off with dessert (tiramisu, anyone?) and the movie.

Is there anything that you regularly promise to your loved ones? Armando has always wanted to see Las Vegas. When we drove from Canada to Mexico, I told him that we didn't have time for the detour. We could have gone if I'd been willing to make the effort. I told him we'd do it "some other time soon." I meant it at the time, but life and other plans crowded in. Now, almost five years have passed—and no Vegas.

On our most recent trip to visit Armando's family in Guadalajara, I promised his darling eight-year-old niece, Arantxa, that I'd play Monopoly with her, and that she could perform her original belly-dance choreographies for me. Again, other priorities crowded in and we ran out of time. No Monopoly, no belly-dance show, and no video night with the other kids, though we'd promised.

A few years from now, I probably won't remember the clothes

we bought on that "necessary" shopping trip downtown, but I will keenly feel the fact that Arantxa isn't that precocious eight-year-old anymore, and never will be. You can always buy more clothes, or make more money, but you can't buy back lost time with your most precious people.

Look at this from another perspective. Do you ever stop to think about what some of your plans for someday might be costing you today? We don't own a home right now, and we'd love to buy our dream house "someday." But if Armando and I make that our primary goal right now, what might it cost us? To save for the down payment, would we end up working twice as hard and spend less time together? Once inside the dream house, would the huge mortgage payments push us to work even harder? Would we play less, laugh less, travel less, and worry more? *In the end, would the house really be worth all of that?*

In survey after survey, people who have it all, or who have a lot, tell us that once you get that "thing" that you wanted so badly, the high soon wears off. You get used to it, and you're soon chasing something else. So it might be a good idea to carefully consider the "somedays" that you willingly trade your todays for—they might not all be worth it.

SILENCE THE VOICE OF SELF-SABOTAGE

If you've read any self-help stuff at all, you've probably heard of what some people call the "inner critic" or "saboteur."

Regardless of what you might call it, it's that voice that shows up just when you're about to start something wonderful. And it seems that the more wonderful or important your goal or plan, the louder that voice gets. Now, before someone decides that I need to take an anti-psychotic medication for my hallucinations, it's important to point out that I'm not talking about actually hearing a "real" voice, out loud. You might experience what I'm referring to as words spoken in your head (as I often do), or it might present itself more subtly, like a strong urge or feeling.

If you have low self-esteem and decide to finally love your physical self just as you are, right now, that voice will show up when you look at yourself in the mirror: "Beautiful? Are you kidding? Just look at that that spare tire—yech!"

As soon as you decide to stop eating emotionally and finally lose that extra weight, that voice will immediately remind you about the box of double chocolate chip cookies in the cupboard. That's part of why I never have any double chocolate chip cookies in my cupboard—I'm not handing that voice any extra ammunition to use against me.

If you want to stick to your new exercise routine, the voice will kick in just as you're about to get off the couch and put on your sneakers. "Are you sure?" it'll ask, seductively. "It's pretty cold outside. Maybe you should wait until tomorrow. Does it matter if you wait just one more day?" Tomorrow the voice will be ready with another excuse, perhaps one even more compelling.

I thought that this was just my own weak will, my subconscious resistance to whatever change I wanted to make, until the day I heard Jim Rohn, the business philosopher I mentioned earlier, talk about the fact that even in his seventies, with all that he's accomplished in his decades as a motivational and inspirational teacher, he still hears that voice every day. It never gives up, always trying to waylay his most important plans and commitments to himself and others.

When I consider Jim's wisdom and his advanced years, it seems to me that we may never be able to make that voice disappear. Stories like Jim's make me suspect that this voice is simply part of the human experience. It will probably never go away, but you can train yourself to ignore it and to do the opposite of what it tells you.

When you make a fabulous plan and then that voice starts to speak—suggesting that you should probably just give up the "stupid" idea, or put things off for another day—ask yourself this: Would listening to this voice, and doing what it suggests, be in my greatest interest? Is this voice really looking out for me, or will I regret it afterwards if I listen? Will I end up breaking a promise to myself, or to others, or let myself down in some way?

I'm not falling for it any more—at least not as much as I used to. If you're determined to create a different life for yourself, one in which you keep your promises to yourself and to others, don't let it win in your life, either.

PREPARE TO BE AFRAID

Usually, when coaching clients first start working with me they're excited. They *know* that the changes that they want to make are exactly what they need to be doing right now.

But once they get started making those changes, the panicky emails start coming. It's so predictable that I'm tempted to start laughing. I don't, because I know that their fears feel very real.

For years, I had the goal of being flown across North America (and the world) for speaking engagements—it's written into my plan for my life in one of my earliest tattered notebooks. When I wrote it, I'd never actually spoken to any group, but somehow knew that it was in my future.

Because of the confidence with which I wrote down the goal, I was totally shocked by my reaction when I received my very first invitation to speak. It was for the biggest women's event in the country, thousands of miles from home, all expenses paid, five-star hotel, everything I'd said that I wanted. I should have been thrilled!

During the three months between being offered the gig and the event itself, I was a wreck. Some days, I felt so jittery that I could hardly write my name with a pen.

I worried that as soon as I opened my mouth it would be disastrously obvious that I'd never given a presentation before. I was sure that my lecture would be boring, that I'd go blank on stage, and that I'd panic at the sight of the crowd. A few days before the talk, a new potential disaster occurred to me and I almost imploded with fear: What if no one showed up?

The big day arrived. I stood up before the crowd, opened my mouth, and my speech came out perfectly. No big surprise there—I'd been practicing it for three whole months! The crowd laughed in all the right places, asked lots of questions, and even took notes. Most amazing of all, so many people showed up that they couldn't close the doors—a crowd of people actually ended up listening from the hallway! Despite the preceding three months of terror, I couldn't wait to do it again. The speech, that is—not the terror.

That experience taught me that it's normal to be terrified when you take a huge step towards a dream. You've probably heard before that the original purpose of fear, and the shaking and nervousness caused by adrenaline, was to protect us from danger. So, when we take that leap forward, and then feel the inevitable fear that follows, we worry that that fear means "Look out! There's danger ahead!"

If you get the opportunity of a lifetime and then start to panic, it's not because your body and mind somehow know that you're going to fail. It's not a premonition that something terrible is going to happen. It's normal. The bigger the opportunity, the bigger the panic. That's just the way it is.

These days, I find it much easier to handle the worry and the trembling when they hit. Instead of working myself into a frenzy of fear, I congratulate myself: "Way to go! You know what this means: You're taking it to the next level! You're out of the comfort zone and heading for your dreams!" Reminding myself of this calms me right down.

The more nervous that you feel about a new step in your life, the more thrilled you'll usually end up being about the outcome. In life, I think that you and I should be more worried if we're *not* feeling nervous on a regular basis. That would likely mean that we're not growing, and that we aren't heading towards our dreams with any kind of meaningful velocity.

MY BLESSING TO YOU

I want you to know how much I've thought of you while writing this book. I hope that it's been just what you needed right now in your life. I hope that throughout these pages, I've opened windows for you through which you've begun to see the wonderful experiences and realities that might be possible in your life.

Though I've shared with you my personal prescription for life, and have shared a lot of myself with you in the process, it's really all about you. Under all the stress, fear, failures, and wrong choices you might have made in your life, you know who you really are, and how you're meant to live.

I hope I've successfully reminded you of how totally original you are, how worthy of love you are, how brilliant and wonderful your body is, and what your body and life need to thrive. Despite the challenges you may have had so far in your relationships, you can start over any time, and become the wonderful partner and friend you truly are. You know what your dreams are, somewhere in your heart, even if you haven't dusted them off in years. You have everything you need to achieve them, and whatever you don't have right now will come to you.

You're naturally creative, you know your most important priorities in life (even if you're not living them yet), and deep down you know what you love, and what makes you feel most alive and connected. You were already more than enough, long before I ever came along.

Bring your plans for "someday" into today. Keep your dreams, values, and priorities in mind all the time, and let them guide you into the choices that will help you create a life that you love.

I send you much love, and I hope that blessings continue to pour down upon your life. May you live a life rich in meaning, health, and happiness!

YOUR PRESCRIPTION FOR HEALTHY EATING

SAMPLE MENU

What I Eat in a Typical Day

SPECIAL NOTE: I specifically decided to mention brand names that I use because I thought it might be interesting and helpful to you to know exactly what I usually eat.

Breakfast (on a busy day!)

Big bowl of cereal
1 cup mixed berries
Fortified soy milk

NOTES

* This simple "bowl" comes completely balanced, as it has carbohydrates, fruit, and protein.

* The cereal might be as simple as some Cheerios (oats are an excellent healthy carbohydrate), oatmeal (real, not instant), or an organic multigrain high-fiber cereal such as Nature's Path Whole-O's. I have a mild wheat allergy, so these are all wheat-free carbohydrate options.

* In spring and summer I'll use fresh berries (organic if possible); the rest of the year I keep a huge bag of Big Valley Mixed Berry Blend from Costco in the freezer (it contains antioxidant-packed blackberries, blueberries, and raspberries) and defrost some every morning in the microwave.

* I use vanilla flavor Silk soy milk because I find it really close to the taste of real milk. I can't drink milk because I also have an allergy to milk protein.

Morning snack

granola bar and an apple

NOTES

* Choosing a good granola bar can be tricky. Some are closer to candy bars, covered with chocolate or a candy-like coating, or overly sweet and sticky. I like Nature Valley plain granola bars (honey oat or apple cinnamon flavor), as they're made from fairly natural ingredients, have few additives, contain oats and some fiber, and don't have a lot of unnecessary extras. They're still sweet, so eating one feels almost like I'm having a cookie.

Lunch (if I'm at home)

1 omega-3 enriched egg (I sometimes have two, or add an extra white), sunny-side up, fried in olive oil
Rice or healthy (low-fat) tortilla chips
Tomato salsa (poured over both the egg and the rice/chips)

NOTES

* You might think that eggs make for a rather strange lunch, but, as I may have mentioned, I'm not a great cook, and I usually need to both prepare and eat fairly quickly. I specifically choose omega-3 fatty acid enriched eggs to increase my intake of these important fats. This meal works because I like it and I can do it in minutes (we usually have leftover rice in the fridge or all-natural healthy tortilla chips in the cupboard), and it's balanced with protein, a carbohydrate, vegetables, and a healthy anti-inflammatory fat.

* Mexican-style salsa is a fantastic "vegetable" source because it's loaded with cooked tomatoes (richer in the antioxidant lycopene than fresh tomatoes), onions, and health-promoting chili peppers. I pile it onto all kinds of different dishes rather than using less-healthy ketchup. My favorite brand is Herdez, as it tastes very close to homemade Mexican salsa and also has no preservatives or additives.

Afternoon snack

I tend to graze throughout the afternoon, depending on when I get hungry and what's available, and usually will eat several things at different times, such as:

A handful of nuts

An orange

A small amount of tortilla chips with lots of antioxidant-rich
hummus and more salsa

A small bowl of Nature's Path Pumpkin Flax Plus granola with fresh
fruit and soy milk

A "power shake" made from soy milk, fruit, flax seeds, and oats

NOTES

* It's always a good idea to vary what you eat from day to day, as that will make it more likely that you get all the different nutrients that your body needs. For example, if I've had soy milk with cereal at breakfast, I might be less likely to have a bowl of granola or a shake with soy milk in the afternoon. You'll also notice that tomatoes appear often during this sample day. The next day, I might deliberately choose some other vegetables, to mix things up.

Dinner

A green salad with chunks of red pepper and tomato, with extra
virgin olive oil and balsamic vinegar dressing (if Armando
makes it, he loves to toss some omega-3-rich walnuts
on top)

Brown rice pasta

Tomato-based sauce (Armando makes a special creation based
on a store-bought all-natural pasta sauce)

Broccoli (stir-fried or steamed, fresh or frozen)

Salmon burger patty or seasoned chicken breast, fried in a small
amount of olive oil

NOTES

* At this very moment, we have big bags of both salmon burgers and chicken breasts in our freezer. Because we're busy people who live on the fly, it's risky to have fresh fish or chicken in our fridge—it might end up going bad! We love frozen food (though not the kind that has had chemical extras added to it).

* One of the biggest excuses I hear for why people don't eat more vegetables is this: "I buy them but they just go bad in my fridge, so they're a waste of money." Frozen vegetables last much longer, are there when you need them, and have actually been shown to often have more nutrients than fresh vegetables (they're frozen right at the source and don't lose nutritional value through travel).

Evening Snack

Could be any one of:

Granola bar
A small bowl of fresh fruit (or a whole fruit such as an apple or pear)
A handful of mixed nuts

• • •

As I've mentioned before, the primary factor that determines when and how much I eat is whether I'm hungry or not. A major reason why I haven't had to worry much about my weight in my adult life is because I learned early on to eat when I'm hungry and stop when I'm full. In the afternoon and throughout the day, the time I have my first snack and how many snacks I end up having are totally determined by what my body asks for. I consciously avoid eating out of boredom, or to procrastinate, or just because it's "time." Listen to your body and then give it good things!

Examples of Healthy Food Choices

(anti-inflammatory foods marked with a *)

Breakfast

PROTEIN
eggs/omega-3 eggs*
milk/fortified soy milk
yogurt
low-fat cottage cheese
smoked salmon*

CARBOHYDRATE
whole grain high-fiber cereal*
oatmeal (not instant)*
high-fiber granola w/nuts*
    (one without dried fruit)
high-fiber bread*

FRUIT/VEGETABLE
berries*
cantaloupe*
tomato salsa*

HEALTHY FAT
ground flax seeds* (rich in
    omega-3)

Lunch

PROTEIN
tuna*
smoked or canned salmon*
sardines*
chicken
hard-boiled omega-3 eggs*
almonds*
nut butters (almond, peanut)*

CARBOHYDRATE
whole-grain high-fiber bread*
brown rice*
quinoa*
hummus*

FRUIT/VEGETABLE
green salad*
tomatoes*
salsa*
avocado*
cucumber*
red/green/yellow peppers*

Lunch (cont'd)

HEALTHY FAT

olive oil*

Dinner

PROTEIN

fish (tuna, salmon)*

chicken

turkey

CARBOHYDRATES

brown rice*

brown rice pasta

whole wheat pasta

FRUIT/VEGETABLE

green salad*

spinach*, broccoli*, kale*

asparagus*

cauliflower*, cabbage*

garlic*

HEALTHY FAT

olive oil*

Low-glycemic fruits for snacks

apples*

cantaloupe*

berries*

grapefruit*

peaches*

High-protein snacks

nuts* (almonds, peanuts, walnuts)

low-fat yogurt

nut bars

QUICK FIXES

Healthy Substitutes
for Everyday Foods

Not Great	Better	Best
Soda Pop	Fruit Juice Bottled Green Tea Drink	Water Green Tea (Real)
White Bread	Whole Wheat Bread	Dense High-Fiber Whole Grain Bread
Salami	Chicken or Turkey Breast Luncheon Meat	Tuna or Smoked/ Canned Salmon
Fried Potato Chips	Baked Potato Chips	Baked Blue Corn Tortilla Chips
Sugary Cereal	Flavored Instant Oatmeal	High-Fiber Whole Grain Cereal Oatmeal
Artificially Flavored Fruit "Gummies"	Dried Fruits	Fresh Berries
Peanut Candy Bars	Processed Peanut Butter	Almond Butter Unsweetened Natural Peanut Butter Whole Nuts

Not Great	Better	Best
Mayonnaise	Low-Fat Mayonnaise	Hummus Tzatziki
Steak	Lean Beef or Chicken	Salmon Steak
Hydrogenated Margarine	Non-hydrogenated Margarine	Olive Oil Spread
Creamy Salad Dressing	Oil-Based Salad Dressing	Olive Oil/Balsamic Vinegar Dressing with Herbs
(Fast-Food) Grilled Cheeseburger	(Fast-Food) Grilled Chicken Burger	(Fast-Food) Grilled Chicken Salad
Jelly	Whole-Fruit Jam	Apple Butter
Ketchup	Mustard	Tomato Salsa
Fries	Plain Baked Potato	Brown Rice
Lard	Vegetable Oil	Olive Oil
Hard Liquor	White Wine	Red Wine
Eggs Benedict	Plain Boiled or Poached Egg	Omega-3 Scrambled Eggs, Stir-Fried with Veggies (one yolk, 2 whites)
White Flour Pancakes	Whole Wheat Pancakes	Multigrain Pancakes With Oatmeal and Chunks of Cinnamon- Sprinkled Apple
Sugar or Syrup	Honey	Agave Nectar (sweet & low- glycemic!)